Leadership Styles

Tony Kippenberger

- Fast track route to mastering effective leadership styles

- Covers the key areas of leadership styles, from developing a style to suit the situation and organizational type to cross-cultural issues and the new interest in 'servant leadership'

- Examples and lessons from some of the world's most successful leaders, including David Simon and John Browne, Konosuke Matsushita and Herb Kelleher, and ideas from the smartest thinkers, including Manfred Kets de Vries, Ed Schein, Gareth Jones and Bob Goffee, Ken Blanchard and John Adair

- Includes a glossary of key concepts and a comprehensive resources guide

LEADING

08.04

essential management thinking at your fingertips

The right of Tony Kippenberger to be identified as the author of this work has been asserted in accordance with the Copyright, Designs and Patents Act 1988

First published 2002 by
Capstone Publishing (a Wiley company)
8 Newtec Place
Magdalen Road
Oxford OX4 1RE
United Kingdom
http://www.capstoneideas.com

CIP catalogue records for this book are available from the British Library and the US Library of Congress

ISBN 1-84112-357-9

Printed and bound in Great Britain

This book is printed on acid-free paper

Substantial discounts on bulk quantities of Capstone books are available to corporations, professional associations and other organizations. Please contact Capstone for more details on +44 (0)1865 798 623 or (fax) +44 (0)1865 240 941 or (e-mail) info@wiley-capstone.co.uk

Contents

Introduction to ExpressExec

ExpressExec is 3 million words of the latest management thinking compiled into 10 modules. Each module contains 10 individual titles forming a comprehensive resource of current business practice written by leading practitioners in their field. From brand management to balanced scorecard, ExpressExec enables you to grasp the key concepts behind each subject and implement the theory immediately. Each of the 100 titles is available in print and electronic formats.

Through the ExpressExec.com Website you will discover that you can access the complete resource in a number of ways:

» printed books or e-books;
» e-content – PDF or XML (for licensed syndication) adding value to an intranet or Internet site;
» a corporate e-learning/knowledge management solution providing a cost-effective platform for developing skills and sharing knowledge within an organization;
» bespoke delivery – tailored solutions to solve your need.

Why not visit www.expressexec.com and register for free key management briefings, a monthly newsletter and interactive skills checklists. Share your ideas about ExpressExec and your thoughts about business today.

Please contact elound@wiley-capstone.co.uk for more information.

Introduction to Leadership Styles

Why is the style of leadership used today so important? Why does it need to be different from the way it's always been done? Chapter 1 explains:

» how the shift from manual to knowledge work has changed what is now required of a leader; and
» why the expectations and aspirations of employees call for a different leadership style.

"Becoming a leader is not easy, just as becoming a doctor or a poet isn't easy, and anyone who claims otherwise is fooling himself."
Warren Bennis, author and leadership expert

It is difficult, at the beginning of the twenty-first century, to grasp the scale of change that has occurred in the workplace over the last 100 years or so. But to understand the vital emphasis that is now placed on leadership, and in particular the style of that leadership, it is valuable to put these changes in context.

When the industrial revolution began at the end of the eighteenth century, it triggered a century of invention. In the process, it created a fundamental shift in the nature of production, from being craft-based to being technology-based. But the changes this brought about in the nature of work were deeply traumatizing and created a huge sense of alienation among a new type of production worker. People were forced, in their search for work, to move from the countryside to the grim, unsanitary conditions of the new industrial towns and cities. It was this alienation that prompted Marx to predict that the capitalist system would collapse. But it didn't. Peter Drucker, the doyen of management scholars, who has been thinking and writing on the subject for 60 years, argues that the credit for this should go to one man – Frederick Winslow Taylor – and his theory of scientific management. "Few figures in intellectual history have had greater impact than Taylor. And few have been so wilfully misunderstood and so assiduously misquoted."[1]

Taylor first began his study in 1881, two years before Marx's death. What prompted him was his own alarm at the growing and mutual hatred between capitalists and workers. What he wanted to do was to increase workers' productivity so that they could earn a decent living – a concept dismissed by his contemporaries, who believed that the only way a worker could produce more was by working longer or harder, or both.

THE PRODUCTIVITY REVOLUTION

Although machinery had vastly increased industrial output, manual workers themselves were no more productive in making or moving things in the late nineteenth century than they had been in Greek and Roman times. By studying time and motion and breaking down every different element, Taylor identified the best way for each manual operation to be undertaken. Within a few years, productivity began to rise at a compound rate of about 4% a year – what Drucker calls the unrecognized productivity revolution. As a result, productivity roughly doubled every 18 years and is now some 50 times higher, in the advanced countries, than it was at the start of the twentieth century. Drucker argues that the consequent growth in living standards had, within a matter of 50 years, converted Marx's proletarians from potential revolutionaries into blue-collar, middle-class aspirants.

When Taylor began his study of scientific management, nine out of ten people were manual workers. Even by the middle of the twentieth century, in all the developed countries, the majority still were. But by 1990 that proportion had shrunk to 20% of the workforce. By 2010, Drucker believes, it will be no more than 10%. This, as he points out, means that the manual productivity revolution is all but over.

THE MANAGEMENT REVOLUTION

To create wealth in the future, what will matter is increasing the productivity of non-manual workers and that, Drucker argues, means "applying knowledge to knowledge" – a process that he places at the heart of what he refers to as the management revolution. Management, as he points out, did not emerge as a discipline until the late 1940s, up until that point organizations were "administered" rather than managed.

A flavor of the time can be caught in a book written in 1950 by William Newman, an early McKinsey consultant, entitled *Administrative Action: The Techniques of Organization and Management*. In it Newman expresses a concern: "Some writers separate the work of top administration from that of subordinates. Unfortunately, there is no agreement on whether the top level should be called management or administration or what is covered by the term selected . . . "

Drucker himself was one of the first to start studying the process of managing during and after World War II. As Drucker points out, at that time a manager was defined as "someone who is responsible for the work of their subordinates" – in other words, "the boss." By the early 1950s, however, the definition had changed to someone who is "responsible for the performance of people."

LEADERSHIP REVOLUTION

Beginning in the 1970s and rapidly accelerating during the 1980s, there has been a further change – one that places leadership in a pivotal role as an essential part of achieving ever better productivity and performance.

The shift from manual to knowledge work in most economies, the rise of living standards and therefore expectations, the growth in educational qualifications and sophistication, are just some of the things that have changed people's attitudes. The workforce of today is a far cry from that of 100 years ago. We live in an age where people have choices, where the deference common in an earlier age has disappeared, where the right to personal self-fulfillment is a widely shared belief.

As a result it is now recognized that, to get the best out of people, they need to be led, not just managed as subordinates. They need to feel motivated, committed, and even inspired. Persuasion, not coercion, is required. Status and position are no longer enough. To get the real results required in a highly competitive age, people need to want to give their best, not just be told to do so.

Autocratic and hierarchical management systems have given way to much more open and democratic ways of managing. Simultane-ously, the reasons why someone should follow someone else's lead have changed markedly. A much more egalitarian society, increases in employee-empowerment, and the flatter nature of many organizations means that leaders now have to "win" followers.

And with this has come a whole new set of requirements for those who aspire to lead their organization – or parts of it – to success. Nowadays, competitiveness between organizations takes place not just at the level of the products and services they provide, but much more deeply at the level of the competences they possess. And nowhere are those competences more critical than in the style of leadership they have. The qualities, attitudes, beliefs, and behaviors of those whose task it is to bring out the best in their people.

NOTE

1 Peter Drucker, *Post-capitalist Society*, HarperBusiness, 1994.

What are Leadership Styles?

Leadership styles are reflected in behaviors and attitudes, but these in turn are the outcome of complex interactions between the way we think and feel. Chapter 2 looks at what this means by:

» explaining how these interactions work;
» providing a definition of leadership style; and
» looking at how far we can adapt our styles, without acting out of character.

"Effective leadership is the only competitive advantage that will endure. That's because leadership has two sides – what a person is (character) and what a person does (competence)."

Stephen Covey, author of The Seven Habits of
Highly Effective People

At one level, the concept of "leadership style" is simple to define: it is the style that a leader adopts in their dealings with those who follow them. Clearly, underlying this is an assumption that there is a "right" and a "wrong" style.

According to the management literature, the appropriate style will depend on a wide variety of criteria, including the relationship between the parties involved, the nature of what needs to be done, and the match or mismatch between the difficulty of the task and the competencies available (see Chapter 8). But this very simplicity masks a much more complex subject.

One of the first questions to ask is what we mean by "style?" Generally, in this type of context, style is taken to mean a way of behaving. But behavior shows itself in many different forms. It can be mannerisms such as the use of voice and the tone and volume employed, or in body language and physical demeanor. It can be *what* we say – words that can vary across the spectrum from aggressive to placatory. It can be in the form of conduct, which may express calmness or agitation.

At a deeper level, behavior can be the loyalty we show, the trust we place, the commitments we make, the honesty and truthfulness with which we deal with others. Taken together, different behaviors are read by others as the way we are acting toward them.

But that is to reach just the outer layer of the complexities – because the way we behave is not just defined by the situation. Behavior is determined by many different things, things that psychologists and psychoanalysts spend their lifetimes seeking to understand. Behavior is an outcome of the interplay between our cognitive side, the way we think and reason, and our emotional side, the way we feel. And our cognitive and emotional responses are themselves a mix of nature (instinct) and nurture (experience). The way we behave is a powerful reflection of our personality and character, the product of the often unconscious processes that are at work within us.

A RECENT DEFINITION

One of the most recent leadership experts to try to define what is meant by leadership styles is Manfred Kets de Vries, a psychoanalyst and professor at INSEAD business school in France. In his 2001 book, *The Leadership Mystique*,[1] he points out that leadership is a *property*, "a set of characteristics – behavior pattern and personality attributes – that makes certain people more effective at attaining a set goal." But it is also a *process*, "an effort by a leader, drawing on various bases of power (an activity with its own skill set), to influence members of a group to direct their activities toward a common goal."

Because leadership cannot take place without followers and always has situational factors that have to be taken into account, Kets de Vries defines leadership style as the point of interaction between three things:

» the leader's character type – their values, attitudes, and beliefs, their position and experience;
» the followers' character types – their values, attitudes, and beliefs, their cohesiveness as a group; and
» the situation – the nature of the task, the life-stage of the organization, its structure and culture, its industry, and the wider socio-economic and political environment.

But, as Kets de Vries explains: "An individual's leadership style – a synthesis of the various roles that he or she chooses to adopt – is a complex outcome of the interplay of that person's inner theater . . . and the competencies that the person develops over the course of their lifespan."

An individual's "inner theater" is made up of their motivational needs, their character traits, and their temperament. These character traits find expression in certain behavioral patterns that can be called personal, cognitive, and social competencies. In Kets de Vries' view, "in any given situation, a certain set of competencies contributes to effective leadership. The challenge for leaders (or potential leaders) is to develop a repertoire of competencies that covers most contingencies."

ADAPTABILITY

This latter point is critical, because inherent in the concept of "leadership styles" is the assumption that an individual can change his or her style at will. Of course, most people are readily capable of changing their outward behavior to fit the circumstances – looking sad, acting happy, or putting on a grim face, as appropriate. To survive in an adult world, and to make headway in most organizations, people learn to become good actors – sometimes acting out of character – to smooth the path where necessary. Human beings, by and large, are also astonishingly adaptable – able to change their normal mode of behavior for quite extended periods where necessary, for example when thrust into an unexpected situation like an emergency.

But the degree to which we can subvert or distort our natural feelings and our instinctive behavior patterns is necessarily limited. Where this does happen for any extended period, we are likely to develop what Kets de Vries describes as a "false self." In his leadership seminars for top executives he finds it not at all unusual to come across people who are seriously out of touch with the way they feel. "Their many years of conformity on the corporate path have blurred the distinction between their own feelings and the feelings that are expected of them." They become "a caricature of the 'good executive'" – a false self. People in this position are unlikely to be able to provide effective leadership.

INTEGRITY

One of the central tenets of effective leadership, repeatedly expressed by most experts on the subject, is the need to act with integrity. It is the key to winning trust and commitment. But integrity is more than just acting honestly and speaking truthfully; it is also being honest about oneself. Hence another principle of good leadership, the need to know and be yourself.

So, you might ask, is the whole concept of "leadership styles" built on a false premise? Even if they can, should people change styles? The answer to both questions is that it is a matter of degree. If one is talking about adapting a chosen style to fit a new and specific set of different circumstances, then this may be utterly appropriate – the most open and democratic leader must be able to switch to issuing highly prescriptive orders in a crisis. On a day-to-day basis, effective leaders shift their style to match the micro-situation, though there needs to remain an underlying consistency if morale and motivation are to be maintained.

But if one is talking about a fundamental change of style that will require out-of-character behavioral changes over the long term, then the answer should be no. How we lead is a reflection of our character, our personality, and our experience. As a result, the range of styles we can properly adopt is inevitably limited. To put oneself in the highly stressful role of leader without acknowledging this reality is to court disaster. Square pegs in round holes don't fit and often get damaged when anyone tries to make them fit.

PERSONALITY TYPES

So, if there is a limited degree to which any of us can adjust our style without becoming untrue to ourselves, how can we recognize our natural style?

There are many psychometric tests now in use that seek to define the type of person we are. One of the best known is the Myers – Briggs® personality type test that also helps to determine our natural "comfort" zones in terms of behavior. More than two million people in the US alone answer its battery of questions each year to elicit their positioning along four different dimensions. At their most simplistic these are: extrovert or introvert; a liking for hard fact and detail or a preference for intuition; a tendency to use head (impersonal) or heart (personal); and quick decision-taking or a desire for a lot of information first. Each of the 16 types that the test produces has its own personality profile which should provide some indication of our preferred leadership styles (see Chapter 9).

PREFERRED ROLES

Other tools help to identify how we are likely to behave, contribute, and interrelate with others in a team environment. Given that leadership nowadays tends to take place in such a context – either at local or top team levels – these can provide important insights. One such is the Belbin® Team Roles Indicator, which identifies those who are action-oriented (the Shaper, Implementer, and Completer-Finisher); those who are people-oriented (the Co-ordinator, Team-worker, and Resource Investigator), and those who take cerebral roles (the Plant, Monitor Evaluator, and Specialist). For more on this, see Chapter 9.

LEADERSHIP TYPES

Over the years, lots of management thinkers have identified different leadership types (and their typical styles). One of the most recent and controversial – and therefore interesting – typologies is that produced by Patricia Pitcher, Professor of Leadership at Canada's longest-established business school, École des Hautes Études Commerciales, in Montreal.

As a result of more than eight years of investigation, she argues that there are essentially three types of leader: the "artist," the "craftsman," and the "technocrat," and each has three subsets.

» The artist is emotional, imaginative, daring, exciting, intuitive, creative, unpredictable, visionary, and entrepreneurial. Like an artist, such leaders challenge our views of the world and conjure up a picture of something new, different, better. (See Herb Kelleher in Chapter 7.)
» The craftsman is well-balanced, realistic, reasonable, steady, responsible, predictable, helpful, honest, and trustworthy. The craftsman learns from experience and enables others to do so by accepting that innovation will bring mistakes. (See David Simon in Chapter 7.)
» The technocrat is cerebral, hard-headed, determined, intense, detail-oriented, uncompromising, and no-nonsense in approach. The technocrat intellectualizes and concentrates on finding the facts and the right way of doing things. (See, as a possible example, Robert Horton in Chapter 7.)

Pitcher suggests that technocrats currently run around 80% of companies and that this is why there is a "leadership crisis" in many of them. Instead, she believes that the inspiring and visionary risk-taker (the artist) has the creativity and intuitive sense of the future that leaders need today.

But perhaps we should let Ken Blanchard, author of the best-seller *The One-Minute Manager* and himself a leadership expert (see Chapters 3 and 8), have the last word. In terms of style, he thinks that the leader of the future will "excel as a cheerleader, supporter, and encourager rather than as a judge, a critic, or evaluator."[2]

KEY LEARNING POINTS

» Style is usually seen as the way we behave and behavior reveals itself in many ways.

» Behavior results from an interplay between what we think and how we feel, and is a reflection of character and personality.

» An effective leadership style must reflect the leader's character type, the followers' characteristics, and the situation.

» Leaders must adapt their style, but should not distort their personality so much that they create a "false self."

» Followers look for integrity, and adopting out-of-character behaviors is easily seen through.

» There are many tools to help people understand their preferred styles and roles.

NOTES

1 Manfred Kets de Vries, *The Leadership Mystique*, Financial Times Prentice Hall, 2001.

2 Ken Blanchard, "Turning the Organizational Pyramid Upside Down," in *The Leader of the Future*, Jossey-Bass, 1996.

The Evolution of Leadership Styles

Heroic qualities are often associated with great leaders, but research shows there is no one set of traits that leaders have. Chapter 3 charts the development of thinking about leadership styles from the start of the twentieth century. It traces:

» the demise of Great Man and Trait Theories;
» the large scale research project of the post-War era; and
» the shift in thinking that has taken place over the last 25 years.

"Leaders come in many forms, with many styles and diverse qualities. There are quiet leaders and leaders one can hear in the next county. Some find strength in eloquence, some in judgment, some in courage."

John W. Gardner, author of On Leadership (1990)

Most of us get our first ideas about what leadership qualities are at an early age. We may not initially see it that way, but through the books we read and the films and television series we watch, we are drawn into the stories, myths, and legends about heroes of an earlier age - Robin Hood, William Tell, Joan of Arc, Davy Crockett. Each nation has them.

Later on, we learn about national histories and thus come across rulers and leaders who have played a significant part in them. Depending on the nature of our education, we also come across leaders of other nations who have left their stamp on history. Many have the label "Great" attached to them - like Rameses and Alexander from ancient history, or Alfred, Frederick, and Catherine from comparatively more recent times. Some have other epithets, like Philip the Good, Richard the Lionheart, or William the Conqueror; some need none - like Napoleon Bonaparte. Around the world, different peoples have their own idealized leaders - like Itzcoatl for the Aztecs and Pachacuti for the Incas.

It is altogether natural, therefore, that we absorb a strong sense of leadership as a mysterious yet highly individual quality that certain great people seem to reveal at portentous moments in history. "Cometh the hour, cometh the man." And indeed it is true that there have been remarkable people throughout history who have made an extraordinary impact on their times. But, taking the world's population through time, they are surprisingly few and far between.

GREAT MAN THEORY

Since, with few exceptions, countries at the beginning of the twentieth century were governed by "the ruling classes" - those born into a suitable aristocratic or elevated station in life - it was entirely in keeping with the times that everyone assumed that the great men of the past had been born to the role. How could it be otherwise?

This formed the basis of what is known as the Great Man Theory of leadership – the widely held belief that only a limited number of people were uniquely endowed with certain abilities and traits that made it possible for them to become leaders. And that these traits could only be inherited, not developed, learnt, or acquired. That this assumption held good until well into the twentieth century is a reminder of just how much has changed in the relatively recent past.

British leadership expert John Adair, a firm believer that leadership can be learnt, quotes from a lecture given to students at St Andrew's University in Scotland, during 1934, to exemplify an archetypal "Great Man view": "It is a fact that some men possess an inbred superiority which gives them a dominating influence over their contemporaries, and marks them out unmistakably for leadership. This phenomenon is as certain as it is mysterious."[1]

SEARCHING FOR LEADERSHIP TRAITS

It was a direct consequence of such views that the earliest research into leadership should be directed at trying to discover the traits, attributes, and qualities that marked such people out. With impeccable logic, since they had to be born with leadership genes, researchers sought to observe recognized leaders and see what gave them their "inborn superiority." Indeed, up until the 1940s, the main work on leadership was specifically directed toward what is known as Trait Theory.

The trouble was that, search as one might, the only commonly held qualities and attributes of such a diverse group of people were also shared by many others who did not become leaders. Gradually, researchers came to accept that, while prominent leaders may be unusually gifted, they do not possess a universal set of leadership characteristics. So Trait Theory, as a way to identify leadership potential, had lost most of its momentum by the time of World War II.

It is estimated that over a 50-year period some 300 trait studies had been conducted. The final nail was driven into the coffin when, in 1948, Ralph Stogdill of Ohio State University completed an investigation into 120 of them. He concluded that leadership was neither a matter of passive status "nor the mere possession of some combination of traits."[2] However, he did identify some factors that seemed to recur in the studies. These included:

» capacity – such as intelligence and judgment;
» achievement – in the form of scholarship or knowledge;
» responsibility – self-confidence and dependability;
» participation – sociability and social adaptability; and
» status – both socio-economic and in terms of popularity.

The problem, as always, is that these highly generic qualities are also widely dispersed throughout the population and just having them does not make anyone a leader. As leadership expert Warren Bennis points out, there is no evidence to suggest that everyone with the capacity to be a leader will become one. Nor can one assume that everyone who takes a leadership position is necessarily a leader.

LOOKING AT BEHAVIOR

As interest in inborn attributes declined, researchers switched their attention to the behavior of leaders – effectively their leadership style. In part this was prompted by a growing emphasis in psychology on "behaviorism."

The starting point was work undertaken in the 1930s at the University of Iowa by German-born psychologist Kurt Lewin – one of the founding fathers of social psychology. Together with his colleague Ronald Lippitt, Lewin had undertaken what came to be seen as a classic study of three leadership styles: an autocratic style, characterized by the tight control of group activities with all decisions being made by the leader; a democratic style, which emphasized group participation and majority rule; and a *laissez-faire* style, which involved very low levels of any form of activity by the leader.

Although this study was actually conducted as a series of laboratory experiments involving adolescent boys – a far cry from a business environment – it had been used to argue the case for a shift from an autocratic to a more democratic style of management. Rensis Likert followed it up in the mid-1940s with further research at the University of Michigan (see "Styles of leadership" in Chapter 8) – this also showed that participative and democratic styles were the most successful.

Meanwhile, at Ohio State University, Carroll Sharple and Ralph Stogdill began a 10-year study into leadership behaviors in 1945. Adopting a heavily statistical approach, they identified hundreds of leader behaviors and then grouped them all into two categories – "initiating" and "consideration" – which they placed at each end of a continuum. Leaders showing consideration behaved sensitively toward people, respected their ideas and feelings, and sought to establish trust. Initiating leaders, conversely, put tasks before people, structured work, defined group roles, set deadlines, and imposed discipline. The results indicated that employees preferred the considerate leader, but work performance results were less clear-cut. It seemed that, at least in the short term, better results were obtained under "initiating" leaders.

Back at the University of Michigan, in 1947, Daniel Katz and Rensis Likert began to study leaders who displayed either an employee-centered or job-centered set of behaviors, but used these as two axes rather than a continuum. A similar set of studies was undertaken at the University of Texas. In reality the differences between all these studies were minimal and the results similar – people preferred employee-centered leaders but performance was as high, if not higher, under job-centered leaders.

As with the earlier Trait Theory, these researchers – largely funded by the federal government and the US armed services – were seeking to identify the best style of leadership. But, as before, they failed to recognize that no single style of leadership is universally appropriate in all situations and environments. As a result, they were disappointed when the ideal behavior patterns they identified did not produce consistent improvements in either group productivity or "follower" satisfaction. The fact that the research, although empirical, had generally been conducted among groups of students under a supervisor who treated them kindly or harshly, did not seem to have affected their judgment that the outcomes were applicable in a wider, business context.

The last flourish of the behavioralists was probably the "leadership grid" suggested by consultants Robert Blake and Jane Moulton in 1961, based on Blake's earlier experiences at oil giant Esso (now Exxon). By measuring a leader's concern for people on one axis and their concern for task on the other, they identified 81 different styles, though for simplicity's sake they focused on just five (see "The leadership grid" in Chapter 8). The significance of their approach was that it accepted the need for many different styles and even allowed for some variability in context. It was also particularly noteworthy for identifying, at such an early date, the value of leading through teamwork.

THINKING ABOUT THE SITUATION

Frustrated by their inconclusive search, academic researchers were then confronted by a new problem. In the post-War era, much of America's best managerial and leadership talent returned from war duties and adopted civilian leadership roles – the most prominent being Dwight D. Eisenhower who, having been Supreme Commander of Allied Forces in Europe, became president of the US in 1953. However, what became obvious fairly rapidly was that not all those who had excelled in the military sphere could translate that success into civilian situations. Clearly, not only was there no universally applicable leadership style, but different behaviors and styles would be called upon in different situations.

In an article in *Harvard Business Review* in 1957, entitled "How to Choose a Leadership Pattern," Robert Tannenbaum and Warren Schmidt suggested that there was a continuum of behaviors available to leaders (see "Continuum of Behavior" in Chapter 8). Based on the autocratic–democratic model, they built in a number of situational elements as variables, such as corporate culture. Although this was a step in the right direction, it has subsequently been seen as a rather simplistic view based on the exercise of authority.

What the researchers were finding was that it was one thing to say that leadership effectiveness depended on the situation, but it was another to be able to identify the different situations. Ten years on, in 1967, Fred Fiedler came up with what is known as the Contingency Model (see Chapter 8).

He took as the variables the relationship between leaders and their subordinates, the nature of the task being undertaken, and the degree of authority the leader had. This significantly widened the situational scope covered by the idea. Unfortunately, Fiedler also developed a test to apply to leaders so that their leadership preferences could be taken into account, and from this he sought to predict leadership effectiveness. Arguments continue about the value of these predictions.

In 1969, Kenneth Blanchard and Paul Hersey took a significant step forward with their Situational Model (see Chapter 8). Significant because they recognized what most other models had ignored – the importance of the "followers." It is, after all, the followers who accept or reject a leader and the leader's effectiveness ultimately depends on how they perform. So they looked at subordinates' willingness and competence as the two main variables. In doing so they evolved four main leadership styles: telling, selling, participating, and delegating.

Again, taking the underlying concepts of willingness and competence as variables, Victor Vroom suggested a decision-making model of leadership styles some years later in 1973 (see Vroom-Yetton Decision Model in Chapter 8). Unfortunately, there are 12 considerations that a leader has to bear in mind, making the model rather too complex to use on an everyday basis.

Also in the mid-1970s Robert House – before embarking on the trail of charismatic leadership (see below) – developed four leadership styles through his Path-Goal Theory (see Chapter 8). He looked at two situational variables: the characteristics of the subordinates and the demands or tasks facing them. He saw it as integral to the leader's job to motivate and satisfy subordinates by, for example, offering performance-related rewards and making sure there were no obstacles in the path to achieving the goals they had been set.

Many of these models – some updated and repackaged – remain at the core of management thinking on leadership styles. The last three in particular remain much in use. But, since their development some 30 and more years ago, the leadership debate has been swept in many other directions.

MORE RECENT IDEAS

Since the publication in 1982 of Tom Peters and Robert Waterman's worldwide bestseller *In Search of Excellence*, the market for management books has become vast and every year it is flooded with texts that cover the subject of leadership. Gone are the vast empirical studies of Ohio and Michigan; in their place are case examples and anecdotes. Many books contain the author's personal views on how to become an effective leader and not a few purport to prescribe successful leadership styles. Unfortunately the range is too vast to detail in this short history, though it is useful to take a very brief look at one or two of the more recent interesting strands in leadership thinking that have developed.

Charisma, vision, transformation

As mentioned above, in the mid- to late-1970s Robert House, currently Professor of Organizational Studies at the University of Pennsylvania's Wharton School, began revisiting the concept of charismatic leadership first put forward by German sociologist Max Weber at the turn of the twentieth century (see Chapters 3 and 6 in *Leadership Express* in the *ExpressExec* series).

A significant amount of effort has since gone into trying to identify the characteristics of charismatic leaders. Essentially they are seen to have a powerful vision, a great deal of self-confidence, a strong conviction that they are right, and an assertive, even dominant, personality. This makes them highly effective in crisis situations or periods of significant change. But it can also make them potentially dangerous – especially if they choose the wrong vision. Either way, "charismatic" may be a style of leadership, but it is not a leadership style you can adopt without charisma!

Coinciding with this renewed interest in charisma, a seminal book, *Leadership*, by political author James MacGregor Burns, was published in 1978. In it, he distinguished between transactional and transformational leadership (see Chapter 8). Its timing was remarkable, coming as it did just as US business confronted the need for massive corporate transformation in the face of deep Japanese inroads into its long-established markets. In a movement that continues today, transactional leaders who lacked vision were soon told to make way for a new breed of transformational leaders capable of reviving corporate America. The study of this very different style of leadership also marked a clear break with the more mundane approach of earlier researchers.

Team leadership

As organizations have tried to demolish internal boundaries and open up their hierarchical functional silos, the use of teams as a means of getting work done has proliferated. This has provided a rich training ground for acquiring and developing leadership skills in a relatively risk-free environment.

However, it has also put a great deal of pressure on many who aspire to leadership because their preferred styles do not fit well with working in teams. One of the earliest proponents of team working and team leadership is John Adair, whose Action-Centered Leadership Model has, since the 1970s, been used to train an estimated two million people worldwide (see Chapter 8).

Empowerment, coaching, mentoring

This shift to more open, flatter organizations has also led to a greater concentration on empowering people to make decisions on their own and an increased emphasis on the leadership role of coach and mentor. See *Coaching and Mentoring* as well as *Empowerment* in *ExpressExec* series.

Servant leadership

Another, less prominent model of leadership, which has been growing in influence more recently, is one proposed by Robert Greenleaf. Described as the originator of the empowerment movement for his work in the 1970s, Greenleaf proposed a leadership style that brought out people's full potential by freeing them up so that they could achieve their best. This different style of leadership now appears to have a growing body of adherents (see Chapter 6).

CONCLUSION

For all that they may wish to, researchers have consistently found the subject of leadership, and leadership styles, difficult to pin down. But there is no "one best way" and it is therefore up to each individual to absorb from the wealth of ideas that are available those that best fit their own personality. As James MacGregor Burns said: "Leadership is one of the most observed and least understood phenomena on earth."

TIME-LINE

These dates are indicative, for example some people still believe in Great Man and Trait Theories.

» **Up to mid-1900s**: Great Man Theory.

- » **1900−48**: Trait Theory.
- » **1930s**: Lewin's research into autocratic, democratic, and *laissez-faire* styles.
- » **1945−60s**: Behaviorist Theory (especially Ohio, Michigan, Texas).
- » **1957−70s**: Situational Theory.
- » **1967−present day**: Contingency Theory.
- » **1970s − present day**: charismatic leadership.
- » **1970s − present day**: team leadership.
- » **1970s − present day**: servant leadership.
- » **1978−present day**: transformational leadership.
- » **1982−present day**: *In Search of Excellence* and thousands of management books on leadership.

KEY LEARNING POINTS

- » The idea of leadership qualities being heroic in nature is absorbed by most people during their childhood.
- » Until the middle of the twentieth century there was a prevailing belief that people were born to be leaders – born to be great (Great Man Theory).
- » The earliest leadership research was therefore into the traits such great people showed (Trait Theory).
- » When this failed to reveal a generic set of traits, researchers began looking at behaviors or leadership styles (behavioral studies).
- » When this proved inconclusive, attention switched to the situations in which leadership needed to be displayed (Situational and Contingency Theories).
- » By the mid- to late-1970s, interest in leadership was dwindling until corporate America felt the impact of Japanese incursions into its markets.
- » A renewed interest, beginning in the 1980s, focused on charismatic, visionary, and transformational leadership – Burns, House, and others.
- » Other concepts have grown in importance over the last 30 years, e.g. team leadership (Adair) and servant leadership (Greenleaf).

» There have also been many other suggestions about suitable leadership styles in the waves of business and management books on the subject in recent years.

NOTES

1 John Adair, *Effective Leadership: A Self-development Manual*, Gower, 1983.
2 Ralph Stogdill, "Personal Factors Associated with Leadership: A Survey of the Literature," *Journal of Psychology*, 1948, **25**, pages 35–71.

The E-Dimension

Organizations have been changed by the digital revolution over the last three decades. Now, information technology, and especially the Internet, are critical to strategy and corporate survival. How does this impact on leadership style? Chapter 4 explores some of the key issues. Among them:

» how leadership style determines the priority attached to IT;
» why electronic communication has its disadvantages; and
» the way our personal use of the Internet can determine the effectiveness of our leadership style.

"To change behavior and unleash new ways of thinking, a leader sometimes has to say, 'Stop, you're not allowed to do it the old way,' and issue a challenge."

Sir John Browne, CEO BP

The revolution in information technologies over the last few decades has had a dramatic effect on organizations in terms of how they operate, how they are designed, and how they are organized. We have moved from pyramidal hierarchies with functional silos to flatter, more networked organizations with fewer internal or external boundaries. It is argued (see Chapter 4 in *Leadership Express* in the *ExpressExec* series) that IT and organizational change are now intertwined in a symbiotic relationship – both shaping each other.

Of course, digital communication is not new (the first e-mail was sent in July 1970), though a true international network – what we now know as the Internet – was not functioning until the late 1970s. But it wasn't until the early 1990s that the World Wide Web began to operate and not until the middle of the decade that its widespread use took off. Even in that short time its impact has been enormous, even if many of its future possibilities are still to be felt. One thing is apparent already – how IT, especially the Internet, is used and applied will increasingly be central to corporate strategy and survival.

In terms of leadership styles, there are two immediate implications. One is the attitudes and behaviors that leaders show toward IT and the Internet – because that will affect how seriously it is taken as an issue – and the other is the leadership style they show in the personal use they make of it.

ATTITUDES AND BEHAVIORS

Michael Earl, Professor of Information Management at London Business School, and David Feeny, Vice-President of Templeton College, Oxford, have addressed the first of these aspects.[1] Although they have looked at the leadership styles adopted by CEOs, their findings apply to leaders at many levels.

Their view is stark: "In the information age, IT issues must be proactively embraced. Unfortunately, most CEOs are ill-equipped for this new world. Indeed, surprisingly few provide the necessary leadership." This is not because of a generation gap, they contend, because many older CEOs have made the necessary transition. It is a matter of attitude and leadership style. They have identified the following seven approaches that leaders take.

1 The Hypocrite. This is the type of leader who espouses the strategic importance of IT but then belies this in the way they act – leaving meetings when the subject is to be addressed.
2 The Waverer. Someone who reluctantly accepts that IT is strategically critical but who avoids making it their own personal priority – refusing to find time to deal with it.
3 The Atheist. The person who simply does not believe that IT has the value attributed to it and makes that view public – decrying IT costs and criticizing the IT function.
4 The Zealot. Someone who is absolutely convinced of its criticality, so much so that they believe they are an absolute authority on what needs to be done, even when they aren't – typically someone with the passion of the recently converted.
5 The Agnostic. A leader who believes that IT is strategically important but doesn't commit to this view, always needing to be convinced before approving investment – won't move without a watertight business case.
6 The Monarch. Believes it is a critical strategic issue and is prepared to make the necessary investment, but hands down responsibility for both strategy and operations to a chief information officer (CIO) and then steps back.
7 The Believer. Recognizes IT as having potential for competitive advantage and by their leadership style demonstrates this belief on a daily basis – devotes quality time to the issues and people involved. (See "Best practice" below.)

Only the last of these archetypes, in Earl and Feeny's view, is fit to lead in the information age because of the way "they translate their beliefs into action, how they live their faith every day, and how they practice what they preach. We suggest that belief drives living and that daily living largely determines the quality of leadership practice."

So what are the leadership styles that such "believers" evince? There are five important aspects.

1 They create a positive hunger for change – because successful development and exploitation of IT means new ways of doing things, venturing into unknown territory, and shaping the future. Typically they therefore set stretch goals that ensure the old ways will not be good enough.
2 They set priorities – often small in number – and ensure that everyone focuses on them over the long term. This is the antithesis of the typical corporate "initiative of the month" that, because of its short time scale, precludes the commitment and focus needed for the type of IT developments that create radical change.
3 They constantly signal their positive belief in the criticality of IT in everything they do or say – both internally and externally.
4 They take their IT leadership seriously and spend quality time on IT issues – thinking, talking, and even writing about them. Their "big picture" has IT at its heart.
5 They work closely with their CIO and develop a good formal or informal relationship with them.

An example of someone who Earl and Feeny see as a real "believer," and someone who evidences it in their leadership style, is Sir John Browne, CEO of BP.

BEST PRACTICE – BP'S SIR JOHN BROWNE

John Browne succeeded David Simon, now Lord Simon, (see Chapter 7) as CEO of BP in 1995, having headed the company's production and exploration division (BPX) for six years. From the start, he has been a believer in the value that IT and the Internet can bring to BP. In 1996, BPX's Virtual Team Network was made available to the rest of the company – a PC-based system incorporating videoconferencing, electronic blackboards, and its own intranet, that allowed the division's engineers around the world to share knowledge and information.

Since then Browne has driven home the message – both internally and externally – that BP is to become a knowledge-sharing, learning organization. "Information technology is wonderful," he says, "because it makes rich exchanges possible without formal structures."[2] When challenged about the benefits of BP's merger with Amoco, he stated that the biggest benefits would probably come from knowledge sharing.[3]

Internally, he intentionally included the choice of a new database management system on the main board's agenda to underline the fact that IT was something all the company's top executives should devote time to. Externally, he gives speeches on the importance of IT and he joined the board of Intel because, he said, "there's plenty Intel can teach us."

In 1998 he told BP's IT function that he expected 25% of BP's profit growth over the next five years to come from exploiting smart technologies – what he describes as "digital business." He sees IT as "not just a service function, or a piece of basic technology, but as an activity which could change the nature of the business itself."[4] Indeed, he argues that "digital technology is helping to shape our strategy."

In the US, BP's downstream business has increased sales by 25% by offering heating oil and diesel through its Website and improving its internal business processes to match. Through Trade Ranger, an oil industry B2B exchange, the company hopes to save $1bn in 2001. Browne also believes that its recent mergers and acquisitions – with Amoco and Atlantic Richfield – would have been difficult to complete without the ability to work online: "If every step forward had required a physical meeting we would be years behind where we are." The same goes for the integration phase following the acquisitions.

But Browne's leadership on IT has meant that there are many other, new applications of IT and the Internet at BP. There are over 100 "peer groups," or communities of interest within BP, people doing the same work – geoscientists, drillers, etc. – but in different locations. Web-enabled, they can share ideas, knowledge, and experience. BP has workrooms with three-dimensional computer screens that allow large teams to work on the same project together. In 2001 BP allowed its shareholders for the first time to cast their votes at the company's annual general meeting via its Website – something he sees as essential for a company with an international shareholding like BP.

"The connected economy," Browne said, "is beginning to give us the ability to create new market-places and to integrate and manage complex systems at a distance and with great precision and speed. It is also giving us the ability to spread and share knowledge instantly."[5]

PERSONAL USE

Ever-increasing use is now made of electronic communication as an integral part of what we do. In many instances, it is coming to replace personal, one-to-one interactions. So, for leaders, the way they use it reflects their leadership style.

Leadership is about motivating people to follow your lead. Communication is a critical part of that and, as such, is a litmus test of the attitudes and behaviors that lie behind it. Recipients always watch how we communicate with them and it is the very ubiquity and ease of use of the new means of communication that presents the greatest potential for problems.

The number of recipients of any communication has grown because people now e-mail their address list, where they would never previously have had time to phone them all. Brevity is a valuable time-saver, but much of the nuance and information is lost. In the time it takes to dash off an e-mail, no account may have been taken of its likely impact on people in other locations, or even other countries (see "Cultural diversity" in Chapter 5). Different technologies have different advantages and disadvantages.

» E-mail – an excellent medium for sending short messages of encouragement to an individual, a highly selective group, or a wider audience. Can be used to get good, rapid feedback. Allows people to read in their own time and absorb contents. But e-mail messages do not all get read by everyone at the same time. They are not suitable for controversial or difficult announcements. In many organizations e-mail is often overused.

» Groupware (e.g. Lotus Notes) – valuable for building and consolidating information and ensuring its dissemination. Allows different levels of access – edit or read only. But can be dry and it is not a highly targeted communications medium.

» Intranet – can provide access to large groups of employees, but highly impersonal and experience shows that once initial interest wears off most intranets have only the same motivational value as in-house magazines and newsletters.

» Group videoconferencing – better than text, though not as good as face-to-face. Tends to be unspontaneous and interactions are a bit formal. Needs big bandwidth to be really effective.

» Desktop videoconferencing – more personal than group videoconferencing, easier to respond to visual clues. Still not as good as face-to-face. Not widespread in most organizations.

The problem with all these technologies is that they are not direct, they are mediated by the technology to a greater or lesser degree. Most of them can be used to support leadership activity, but are poor vehicles to initiate or sustain it alone. The biggest problem is that they are weak transmitters of feelings, emotions, and visual clues.

EMOTIONAL INTELLIGENCE

In 1995, a writer for the *New York Times*, Daniel Goleman, wrote his bestseller *Emotional Intelligence* and introduced the importance of emotion in the business environment. In essence, emotional intelligence means understanding your own emotions, learning how to manage them, and then learning to recognize and deal with other people's emotions. It is increasingly recognized as a key ingredient in effective leadership.

If you understand and know yourself, you can find ways to manage your own emotions; recognizing anger, frustration, and pain for what they are and then learning to mitigate their effects and their impact on others. The next step is to empathize with others and learn how to put yourself in their shoes. Once achieved, sensitivity to situations and influencing skills can grow dramatically.

As Manfred Kets de Vries points out, our IQ does not develop much after our teenage years, but our EQ (emotional quotient) goes on developing throughout our lives. And, as he warns, the higher up in an organization we get, the more important emotional intelligence becomes, and technical skills become less important. In his experience, people with high emotional intelligence:

» have better interpersonal relationships;
» are good at motivating themselves and others; and
» are more innovative and creative.

Unfortunately, as Kets de Vries points out,[6] the scar tissue built up on an upward corporate path means that many leaders have lost touch with their own emotions. What they actually feel and what they are expected to feel have blurred. Perhaps it is these corporate scars that account for the endless stories of the use of new technologies, like e-mail, to demotivate people on a large scale by their crass misuse. Harsh, blunt, rude messages, fired off in the heat of the moment can do untold damage. At its extreme, there are examples of people being fired by e-mail – a complete negation of any leadership qualities.

Conversely, there are excellent examples of how Internet technology can be used to good effect in a leadership context. Marjorie Scardino is chief executive of Pearson PLC, the education and media group that owns, among other businesses, the *Financial Times*. The first woman CEO of a FTSE-100 company, American-born Scardino has a flamboyant leadership style, and is described as "a very good leader and very charismatic" by Pearson's director of people and *FT* chairman David Bell.

On the very first day that she took over as CEO, in 1997, she sent staff throughout the Pearson group an e-mail addressed to "Dear Everyone." She used it to introduce herself and signed it Marjorie. Initially this was seen as typically American and "folksy" among a skeptical, heavily media-oriented, workforce. However, since then she has consistently used the same "Dear Everyone" format to inform all Pearson's staff about any major corporate decisions and to disseminate motivational messages. She is now universally known as Marjorie and has won hearts and minds by personally responding to all e-mails she receives.

This, now well-established, pattern of communication enabled Scardino to produce what must rank as an outstanding example of inspirational and motivational leadership on September 11, 2001. When the twin towers of the World Trade Center in New York were hit by the two hijacked Boeings, her thoughts went not only to the 64 Pearson staff in the towers, but also to all of the group's 28,000 employees, many of whom are based in the US. Recognizing the effect that the terrible events would have on people everywhere, she sent the following e-mail:[7]

> "Dear Everyone
> I want to make sure you know that our priority is that you are safe and sound in body and mind. Be guided by what you and your families need right now. There is no meeting you have to go to and no plane you have to get on if you don't feel comfortable doing it. For now, look to yourselves and your families, and to Pearson to help you any way we can.
> Marjorie"

This display of emotional intelligence, showing intense sensitivity to the situation, made maximum use of new communication technologies to reach Pearson employees almost instantly everywhere around the world. It is a classic case of effective leadership.

KEY LEARNING POINTS

» Over the last 25 years, the IT revolution has already made huge changes to organizations and the way they work.
» The importance of digital communication – and especially the Internet – now mean that the way they are used will be central to strategy.
» Leadership behaviors – how technology is perceived and used – will therefore be central to corporate survival.
» Leadership styles determine how seriously organizations judge the importance of these issues.

> » Many leaders fail to provide the necessary leadership – Earl and Feeny.
> » By constantly emphasizing, both internally and externally, the criticality of new information technologies, leaders can achieve big shifts in perception – Sir John Browne.
> » Many new communication technologies are weak transmitters of feelings, emotions, and visual clues – all important elements of effective leadership.
> » So the personal use of technology is critical – Marjorie Scardino.

NOTES

1 Michael Earl and David Feeny, "How to be a CEO for the Information Age," *Sloan Management Review*, Winter, 2000.

2 Steven Prokesch, "Unleashing the Power of Learning: An Interview with British Petroleum's John Browne," *Harvard Business Review*, September–October, 1997.

3 Michael Earl and David Feeny, "How to be a CEO for the Information Age," *Sloan Management Review*, Winter, 2000.

4 Sir John Browne, speech on "Leadership in the New Economy" given at Templeton College, Oxford, May 1, 2001.

5 Sir John Browne, BBC Reith Lecture, 2000.

6 Manfred Kets de Vries, *The Leadership Mystique*, Pearson Education, 2001.

7 Jeremy Warner, "Can she do the business?", *The Independent*, October 20, 2001.

The Global Dimension

Globalization exposes more and more leaders to different cultures. What does this mean for the appropriate leadership style to adopt? Chapter 5 looks at the challenges that leading in different cultures can present. These include:

» understanding cultural diversity;
» expectations of leadership in different cultures;
» different examples of cultural leadership styles; and
» what happens when differences are ignored.

"The more economic barriers come down, the more you see cultural barriers going up."

> *Kevin Barham and Stefan Wills, "Management Across Frontiers," 1992, Ashridge Management Research Group*

If there is one overriding conclusion from the vast amount of research that has been conducted into leadership styles over the last half century (see Chapter 3), it is that the choice of appropriate style should be determined by the situation in which it is to be employed. This requires judgments to be made across a raft of possible variables. If this appears complicated enough, it is as nothing compared to the complexities that arise the moment one steps out of one's own national culture.

As globalization has grown over the last 20 to 30 years, so has the exposure leaders have had to very different views and attitudes. What works in one culture often backfires in another, what is crystal clear in one situation is completely misinterpreted in another. So, if leaders are going to have to adjust their style, they need to understand some of the underlying reasons for this.

CULTURAL DIVERSITY

Management consultants Fons Trompenaars and Charles Hampden-Turner have spent 15 years studying cultural diversity. In their 1999 book *Riding the Waves of Culture*,[1] they explain some of the dimensions that create cultural differences, including five that affect personal relationships.

Relationships and rules

A universalist, or rule-based, culture tends to operate on the basis of standards and codes with an expectation that everyone knows what they are. A particularist, or relationship, culture pays far more attention to the obligations of relationships – be it friend, colleague, or partner. Because relationships are so important, someone from such a culture would not feel it unusual to lie for a friend if the circumstances demanded it. Someone from a universalist culture would automatically believe that it wasn't right to lie – whatever the circumstances.

The application of rules and procedures to ensure consistency is high in many Western countries, where legal contracts are often seen as more important than personal relationships. Countries likely to be more particularist include those in Asia and South America.

In terms of leadership, those in universalist countries should be aware that particularists will resist changing their own local behaviors, indeed they will use them as a basis to create greater solidarity in the face of edicts from head office. Unsurprisingly, there tends to be greater commitment between leader and led in particularist countries where the strong sense of relationship creates powerful reciprocal bonds.

The group and the individual

Cultures differ in the way they put the individual or the group first. Individualist societies, particularly those in Canada, the US, and Denmark, believe that individuals should have as much freedom as possible. In Mexico, Japan, Brazil, China, and France, there is a much greater emphasis on a communitarian spirit that puts the achievement of common goals and objectives ahead of individual freedom and development.

Leadership style can be seriously affected by these preferences. People from communitarian cultures will want to put forward a negotiating team who act as delegates for those they represent, in an individualist culture a single representative may feel free to conduct negotiations on behalf of others. This attitude can also show itself in terms of status – an unaccompanied businessman or woman may be deemed unimportant in a country like Thailand.

In group cultures, decision-taking processes can be extended as everyone tries to reach consensus, but the decision when it comes is likely to be more stable than one decided in an individualistic culture.

Neutral versus emotional

People within a neutral culture seek to keep their emotions in check, seeing any outward display of emotion as inappropriate. This is the case in Japan, China, Indonesia, Austria, and Poland. Those within more emotional cultures show feelings plainly, through laughter, gesturing, and even visible displays of anger. Obvious examples are the ''Latin'' countries of Spain, Cuba, Venezuela, Italy, and France. The UK and the US fall halfway between the two.

In terms of leadership style, clearly recognizing and respecting these differences is critical. But there are a number of related issues that should be borne in mind. For example, the British use humor to release emotional tensions and are quite likely to start a meeting or a presentation with a joke. But not all cultures find this acceptable – for instance the Germans are uncomfortable with jokes in a professional setting, certainly not until people know each other well.

Verbal communication is another problem area. Anglo-Saxons wait for the speaker to finish before talking, whereas voluble Latins interrupt each other – simply to show how interested they are in what the other is saying. Conversely, people from the Far East leave pauses between each part of a conversation, as a mark of respect for what they've just heard, a silence that can easily be misinterpreted as a failure of communication.

In some neutral societies, like Japan, speaking calmly in a flat tone of voice is a sign of respect, whereas Latin societies see big variations in pitch and tone as a way to express enthusiasm. Non-verbal communications also matter – none more so than eye contact. In Italy, extended eye contact carries no particular meaning, in the US and the UK it needs to be very short unless you know each other. In Curaçao it's a sign of respect, in nearby Surinam it's a sign of disrespect.

Specific versus diffuse

In a specific culture, people keep their work and non-work lives apart. They are therefore relaxed about adopting different roles in the two spheres – for example, meeting a more junior colleague from work on a golf course and deferring to them as the better golfer. People from specific cultures make friends readily, because they have many different, context-related relationships – at the gym, in a pub or bar – that don't carry over into other aspects of their lives. They have a large "public" space and a relatively small "private" space in their lives.

In a diffuse society, the position someone holds at work diffuses into his or her personal life and so their authority continues and they are usually deferred to wherever they go: "Herr Doktor Müller is Herr Doktor Müller at his university, at the butcher's, and the garage." People from diffuse societies are more cautious about making friends because once a relationship is developed it carries over to the rest of their lives. They have a small "public" space and a large "private" space in their lives – once admitted to the private space you are a close friend.

From a leadership perspective, the problem arises when people from the two cultures meet. Americans may find Germans remote and difficult to get to know. Germans see Americans as friendly and talkative, but superficial. More seriously, there are also issues of losing face. Specific cultures, with a large public space, are happy to conduct fairly direct interchanges – often preceded by "don't take this personally, but . . . " Diffuse cultures are highly sensitive to criticism aired publicly.

Status – achieved or ascribed

All societies have hierarchical pecking orders. However, they differ in how they accord status. An achieved status is one based on achievement – what you've done. An ascribed status is given by virtue of class, age, gender, and/or education, and refers to who you are.

Respect conferred according to one's family background is considerably higher in places such as Saudi Arabia, Thailand, and India, than it is in the US, Finland, Denmark, and Norway.

For leaders, this is a potential minefield. Getting status wrong can be catastrophic. In many cultures, for example Japan, those with real status are not always visibly separated from those who demur to them. In some cultures age is critical and fielding young whizz-kids is an insult – as the authors put it: "Do these people think they have reached our own level of experience in half the time? That a 30-year-old American is good enough to negotiate with a 50-year-old Greek or Italian?"

The pitfalls that ill-informed leaders can fall into in the new global market-place are legion. To survive, they have to recognize that the style they may have used to date may be inappropriate in a different national or cultural context.

CULTURAL LEADERSHIP STYLES

Since leaders wish to get the best out of those working for them, it is also critical to recognize the style that people from different nationalities will expect. Leadership expert Manfred Kets de Vries identifies five different cultural styles of leadership.[2]

Consensus Model

This is found in countries where making decisions on a group basis is a core cultural value – where there is a long tradition of involving others in the process. Countries where this is expected include the Scandinavian countries, the Netherlands, and Japan.

Charismatic Model

Some countries expect their leaders to take charge. They want them to act with decisiveness, flair, and high visibility. This is a style often expected in Anglo-Saxon countries like the UK, Australia, and the US, as well as South America.

Technocratic Model

This is a structured approach to decision making with organizational processes carefully designed to provide checks and balances. Kets de Vries points out that this style is typically found in Germanic countries (where the word for leader is *führer*) and reflects the different decision-making models introduced after World War II. Leaders will be expected to follow structured and agreed organizational processes.

Political Process Model

This style, which, as the name implies, depends on political processes in decision taking, is found in cultures where complex power networks exist, particularly France – where graduates from the *Grandes Écoles* hold many prominent and influential positions (see also "Elitist" below). Leaders are expected to show consummate political skills (see "Best practice" below).

Democratic Centralism Model

This is cultural style based on two conflicting ideas: that everyone should be involved in discussions and have a say in who is the leader (democracy), yet when the leader then makes decisions, little opposition is allowed (centralism). Kets de Vries points to Russia and other former Soviet Bloc countries as places where this approach is common. It is also, he suggests, found in the Middle East, in countries such as Kuwait and Saudi Arabia. Leaders advocating empowerment in such a culture may receive blank looks.

EUROPEAN LEADERSHIP STYLES

In the mid-1990s the UK's Cranfield School of Management carried out a survey into senior executives in over 2600 companies across eight European countries. The research revealed four different styles.[3]

Inspirational

Similar to Kets de Vries' Charismatic Model mentioned above, this leadership style tends to be both charismatic and future-focused. The leader is individualistic and dominant, allowing key people involved to give their views but, once the necessary information and views have been heard, decision making is clear-cut. It is a pragmatic style that aims to "make things happen" and so has a low tolerance of conceptual thinking. The research showed that it predominated amongst Spanish, UK, and Irish companies, although the style is also present in a significant percentage of Finnish and Swedish organizations.

Elitist

The predominant style in France, where the *Grandes Écoles* play such a part in French business culture. Half the managers in the survey had been to a *Grande École* and a quarter had a further, higher degree as well. Perhaps unsurprisingly, therefore, 83% of French respondents showed a preference for conceptual debate, compared with only 3% of their Swedish and 1% of their UK, Spanish, and Austrian counterparts.

Elitist leaders display mastery of grand theory to gain credibility as strategists and any debate tends to be individualistic. However, in keeping with Kets de Vries' Political Process Model (see above), while full discussion occurs at meetings, the real decisions are not necessarily taken there, or even by those attending. Instead they are often renegotiated, usually in private. But, once a decision has been made, direction is top-down, with little scope for argument or feedback.

Consensual

In the main, Swedish and Finnish companies prefer open discussion with minimal constraint, although some Irish, Spanish, and UK companies share this style. Reaching consensus is a core value, achieved through sharing information and participating in discussions. It is a systematic approach that avoids surprises.

Directive

German and Austrian companies scored highest for this style. Leaders tend to establish the agenda and determine the best way to address issues; and although dialog can be assertive, management can be highly sensitive to feedback. This can lead to known problems being submerged if they are seen as too difficult to raise. Overall, it is a top-down leadership style.

CONCLUSION

Anyone who believes that they can step out of their own national culture and apply the same leadership style on a global stage, even though it has brought them success hitherto, has another thing coming. There is much to be wary of!

BEST PRACTICE – EURO DISNEY TO DISNEYLAND® PARIS

When, in March 1987, France beat Spain to win Disney's first theme park in Europe, Disney's chairman Michael Eisner brought in fellow American Robert Fitzpatrick as the venture's CEO. Having run the Los Angeles Olympics in 1984, Fitzpatrick had the advantage of being a French speaker who knew Europe well and had a French wife.

Disney was determined not to make the same mistake it had made with Tokyo Disney where, as licensor rather than owner, it received only a small part of the earnings. In Europe, it would own, control, and run the park, just 20 miles outside Paris. To do so, it transplanted its Florida management systems – from dress code manual to human resource policies – and appointed Americans to senior positions, such as personnel director Thor Degelman, who had worked at Disney for 25 years. Eisner involved himself personally, removing a $200,000 staircase because it spoilt the view and insisting on installing open fireplaces.

From the start, Disney managers hit problems. At the launch of the company's shares on the Paris Bourse in 1989 Eisner was pelted with eggs. Local farmers protested at the loss of land, trade unions at the infringement of labor laws, and many members of the French establishment scorned what they saw as cultural imperialism. Theater director Ariane Mnouchkine termed it a "cultural Chernobyl" – a phrase that stuck.

When, on April 12, 1992, Disneyland® Paris opened to a great fanfare, only 50,000 visitors arrived compared to the antici-pated 500,000. The inaugural ceremony – being broadcast to five national television networks – was interrupted when a large elec-tricity circuit was sabotaged and signposts to Marne-La-Vallée, the site of the park, were painted over. As the year went on, instead of the 60,000 visitors a day only 25,000 were arriving (of whom less than a third were French). At one point, the company was losing close to $1mn a day.

In January 1993 Fitzpatrick announced that he was stepping down and that Philippe Bourguignon, a Frenchman who had been vice-president of real estate at Euro Disney SCA, would replace him. Bourguignon, who had previously worked with French hotel group Accor for 14 years, set out to turn the business round.

Fitzpatrick – good creatively but weak operationally – had become caught in the middle between Disney in the US and the realities in France. He tried to warn Disney executives that Paris was not like Florida, but his words fell on deaf ears. French colleagues and outside suppliers found Disney management's style insensitive, overbearing, and arrogant – "do as we say, we know best."

Although the American management had changed the content of the attractions to appeal to European traditions – for instance, using the Grimm Brothers' fairy tales and Alice in Wonderland as themes – pricing and expectations were based on the American model – high entry fees, fast food, no alcohol, merchandise sales, and multi-day visits. In fact, European visitors, especially the French, didn't like the prices, came for day visits, ate a leisurely lunch, expected to be able to buy wine and beer, and avoided buying Dumbo pencil cases. Bourguignon cut entry prices by 20%, introduced new hotel packages, sold cheap evening entrance tickets, and introduced better quality merchandise. He also began the sale of wine and beer.

Within weeks of Disneyland® Paris opening, there had been labor problems, with at least one mass walkout. Among other grievances was the fact that managers insisted on the use of English at meetings and enforced a strict dress code – something that is banned by French law. Disney's 13-page manual on dress code – designed to create an "all-American look" – specified earring size, forbade dyed hair, specified finger nail length, and even the types of underwear to be worn. Sensitive to the cultural clash, Bourguignon shifted from American to French working practices – setting a maximum working week, annualizing hours worked, and reclassifying jobs using standard French classifications.

In marketing terms, Euro Disney's advertising had previously promoted the park's size – this had translated into typical American "bigness." Bourguignon shifted instead to using Disney characters popular with Europeans – like Zorro and Mary Poppins – and played up "the Disney magic." In PR terms, he devoted his energies to smoothing ruffled Gallic feathers, including changing the name from Euro Disney to Disneyland® Paris.

Although the company made a large loss in 1994, by 1995 its profit was $22.8mn. Since then it hasn't looked back. Organizations and their leaders ignore cultural differences and sensitivities at their peril.[4]

KEY LEARNING POINTS

» Globalization introduces many new complexities to the existing variables about an appropriate leadership style.

» What works in one culture backfires in another, what is crystal clear in one situation is misinterpreted in another.

» There are five main dimensions that create cultural differences – Trompenaars and Hampden-Turner.

» To survive, leaders have to recognize that the style they may have used to date may be inappropriate in a different national or cultural context – Trompenaars and Hampden-Turner.

» A real issue is the style that people in different cultures expect from a leader. There are many different expectations – Kets de Vries.

» In Europe alone there are four different styles of leadership among senior executives – Cranfield research.

» Previous success is no guarantee of future success if leadership styles fail to take account of deep cultural differences – Euro Disney.

NOTES

1 Fons Trompenaars and Charles Hampden-Turner, *Riding the Waves of Culture*, Nicholas Brealey Publishing, 1999.

2 Manfred Kets de Vries, *The Leadership Mystique*, Financial Times Prentice Hall, 2001.

3 Andrew Kakabadse and Andrew Myers, "Boardroom Skills for Europe," *European Management Journal*, Vol. 14, No. 2, 1996.

4 Lyn Burgoyne, "Walt Disney Company's Euro Disneyland Venture," 1995 (www.hiddenmickeys.org/Paris/English/LynEuroDisney.html).

The State of the "Leadership Art"

There are many ideas and concepts about appropriate leadership styles. The common thread is the importance of the situation in which leadership is to be displayed. What are some of the issues? Chapter 6 includes:

» five different styles that CEOs adopt;
» the importance of knowing the organization's maturity;
» understanding the nature of the organization;
» the differences between feminine and masculine leadership styles;
» the growing interest in servant leadership; and
» some suggested "tricks of the trade."

"If somebody said to me, Herb, I'd love to be a great coach or a great leader but I don't have the time to do it, my response to them would be, you don't have time to do anything else until you accomplish that."

Herb Kelleher, CEO Southwest Airlines

Leadership expert Warren Bennis put it well when he described leadership as "an endless subject, endlessly interesting because it is impossible to get your conceptual arms around it." With thousands of books and tens of thousands of articles on the subject, the debate about it shows no sign of slowing down. What follows are some ideas and concepts about leadership style seen from a number of different perspectives. We look at research findings that suggest there are just five basic styles that CEOs adopt. We consider how leadership styles need to differ to take account of organizational maturity and then how different organizational types make different demands. We then look at the role of gender – are women's leadership styles different? Are they more in keeping with the times? We also look at the leader as servant – a concept that is suddenly growing in popularity. Finally we review what might be called four tricks of the trade that effective leaders use in their leadership styles.

CEO LEADERSHIP STYLES

In the mid-1990s, consultants at Bain & Co ran a research program called "Maximum Leadership" in which they interviewed over 160 CEOs about their leadership style. Somewhat to their surprise, they found just five basic approaches.

» The strategic approach – although strategy is traditionally seen as a core part of the CEO's role, Bain found that only 20% of their sample followed this style. Typically, they see themselves as having the necessary overview of the whole organization and use consultants and outside sources to help garner a wide variety of information on new ideas, economic developments, customer trends, competitors, etc. Because they can spend up to 80% of their time acquiring and analyzing such information, they find other people to run the business for them on a day-to-day basis so that they can concentrate on deciding a long-term strategic goal and then determining how to get there.

» The "human-assets" approach – a style used by around 22% of the sample. These CEOs believe that strategy formulation is for those closest to the markets and the customers – for example, in the business units. So they focus on the values, behaviors, and attitudes they regard as essential for success. This means they spend most of their time in personnel-related activities, concentrating on the growth and development of individuals. They undertake performance assessments and appraisals themselves, they personally recruit and cultivate people, and spend time on career mapping, training, and succession planning. Typically they spend a great deal of their time out of the office – as much as 90% – visiting operations, plants, subsidiaries, and just talking to people to make sure there is a strong congruence on values, standards, and objectives.

» The expertise approach – these CEOs (15% of the sample) see their most important role as the identification and development of expertise or core competencies that will give the business its competitive advantage. They concentrate on the expansion of these capabilities and their dissemination across the organization. To do so they devote their time to studying new technologies, beefing up R&D, analyzing competitors' offerings, and talking to engineers and customers. They recruit those with proven expertise in the appropriate area and use reward structures and other ways to reinforce the message. They tend to be highly focused competence evangelists.

» The "box" approach – this was the largest group in the sample, with 25%. Those CEOs following this style of leadership see the value they add as the systems they create that bring consistency and predictability across the business. The "box" in this context is the controls – procedural, financial, and cultural – that they set and the rules to which all employees must conform. Such CEOs see their primary role in developing, communicating and then closely monitoring such controls so that both behaviors and outcomes fall within clearly defined boundaries. Their day-to-day attention is fixed on exceptions – missed monthly targets or overshot deadlines – all of which they follow up relentlessly. Typically, such CEOs operate in highly regulated industries, or those in which safety is a big issue, where there is little margin for error.

» The change approach – about 18% of the sample, these CEOs focus less on where the organization is going, but concentrate instead on the process of getting there. They take on the role of change agent, pushing through new approaches and different ways of thinking. They seek radical change and are therefore the antithesis of the "box" CEO, seeing control systems and procedures as little more than stumbling blocks to the change they want to make. Up to 75% of their time is spent making speeches, holding employee meetings, and using other forms of communication to motivate people to change. They spend their days meeting customers, suppliers, and employees at all levels.

Clearly, there is inevitably some overlap between these approaches – virtually every CEO mentioned strategy as part of their role. But Bain's research showed that generally CEOs focus on one (or sometimes two) approaches and that when a CEO tries a bit of each, then confusion, lack of effectiveness, and demotivation among employees is the result.

Each of these styles is highly recognizable, revealing as they do the beliefs, attitudes, and predilections of each of the leaders interviewed. The unanswered question is whether they are appropriate for the organization they lead.

STYLES FOR STAGES

Edgar Schein, emeritus professor at the Sloan School of Management, points out that one of the reasons there are so many leadership theories is that different researchers focus on different, often single, elements of a highly complex subject.[1] So, in their own way, each may be right. But many of them ignore organizational dynamics, "particularly the fact that organizations have different needs and problems at different stages in their evolution;" in particular, from Schein's perspective, different *cultural* needs.

He divides the life cycle of the organization, and therefore the kind of leadership required, into the following four phases.

» Creating – here the leader is *animator*, breathing life and energy into the new enterprise and the people working in it. Leadership is about making mistakes but also having the vision and confidence to learn from them.

» Building - at this stage, the leader becomes the *creator of culture*. The entrepreneur's beliefs, values, and assumptions are transferred to the people working in the organization. With success, the leader becomes a role model and their "entire personality becomes embedded in the culture of the organization" (see sections on Herb Kelleher and Konosuke Matsushita in Chapter 7). The individual's strengths and weaknesses become the organization's strengths and weaknesses. The systems and processes become "the way we do things round here" – something that, of course, can become dangerously change-resistant in the future.

» Maintaining - often the most difficult phase, this requires a leader who is a *sustainer of culture* (or those parts of it that remain relevant). As successful organizations grow they attract competition, so they have to become both more effective and efficient. Typically, this is where the "founder-builder" runs into problems of letting go. He or she may even resist the evolution of a new generation of leaders that are needed for a different kind of future. If a new leader (CEO) is brought in, they have to understand the culture, keeping the good (institutionalizing it), and shedding what is no longer appropriate. Schein believes that two elusive qualities are needed: judgment and wisdom.

» Evolving - here the leader is *change agent*. Such is the speed of change that strengths that have been institutionalized can become liabilities. In order to bring about change in an ossifying organization, the leader must help people unlearn things that no longer serve the organization well. This unlearning provokes anxiety, defensiveness, and resistance to change among employees. Schein argues that "the critical thing to understand about cultural dynamics is that leaders cannot arbitrarily change culture in the sense of eliminating dysfunctional elements, but they can *evolve* culture by building on its strengths while allowing its weaknesses to atrophy over time" (see section on David Simon in Chapter 7).

Sometimes, however, a leader has to have the courage to take more radical action - to "bite the bullet" and get rid of the elements of the culture that are inhibiting the kind of growth and change that are needed. This might involve massive restructuring, even replacing the top layers of management. Schein argues that the transformational leader (see Chapter 8) is in a similar position to the original entrepreneur, creating a new organization with new procedures but, he warns, they need to deal with the anxieties and guilt of the employees that remain. "Rebuilding their motivation and commitment often requires higher levels of animation than building an organization in the first place."

ANOTHER ANALOGY

Other analogies of the styles required at different stages of an organization's development have been suggested from time to time. For instance, that a new venture needs a "champion" to fight for and defend the seedling business. The champion wins orders, finds good employees, and displays many (and different) leadership abilities. In its growth phase it needs a "tank commander" who can bulldoze new ideas through and drive the business into the readily exploitable parts of its markets. As it reaches maturity, it needs a "housekeeper" to ensure efficient and economic management of the business through planning and cost control, as well as the careful cultivation of its existing resources. Finally, in decline, it needs a "lemon-squeezer" who gets the maximum out of the business while trying to inject new zest into it – the lemon-squeezer must be tough *and* innovative.[2]

It was Austrian economist Joseph Schumpeter who first described the "gales of creative destruction" as an integral part of capitalism – the necessary and inevitable death of old companies to make way for the new. The constant cycle of birth, growth, maturity, and decline. Indeed, in many developed economies the small and medium-sized company sector now accounts for an ever-increasing proportion of GDP and employment. So debate on the leadership needs of organizations at different stages in their development is likely to continue and grow.

ORGANIZATIONAL TYPES AND THEIR NEEDS

Robert Goffee, a professor at London Business School, and Gareth Jones, visiting professor at INSEAD in France, have also looked at organizations, their culture and their different needs, though from a different viewpoint

By using two cultural yardsticks – sociability (a people-centered, friendly approach) and solidarity (a drive toward shared objectives and unity of purpose) – they have identified the following four organizational character types, each of which needs leaders with different styles.[3]

» The networked organization (high sociability, low solidarity) – an organization where teamwork and knowledge sharing are commonplace needs a leader with excellent interpersonal skills and emotional intelligence. Someone who sees each employee as an individual and treats them as such. Someone who collects soft data about people's motives, capabilities, and values and is attuned to what is going on around them. A leader who uses the internal networks and makes time to talk to people throughout the organization.

» The mercenary organization (high solidarity, low sociability) – an archetypal 1990s organizational form, whose leader's style is typically highly focused and tough. Someone who constantly pushes for high performance. They know what the goals are, put measures in place, hold people to account, and like straight talking. Relationships, for them, are usually kept out of working hours.

» The fragmented organization (low solidarity, low sociability) – typically an academic institution or a professional service firm, such as accountants or management consultants. Leaders here have a tough role. To be effective, their style needs to remind everyone of their obligations to the business and to encourage at least a minimal amount of sociability – neither of which are easy when the leader is often only first among equals or, in some of their colleagues' views, not even that.

» The communal organization (high sociability, high solidarity) – this is an organization type that is not easy to lead, because the high sociability and solidarity can conflict: nobody wants to rebuke or fire a friend. Neither is it an easy organizational type to sustain because it will tend to go one way or the other (i.e., toward networked or mercenary). Good communal leaders tend to have an inspirational leadership style, able to motivate and win the intense loyalty of employees to their vision for the organization. They have to win hearts *and* minds for the organization to stay high on both axes.

Bearing in mind that square pegs don't fit easily into round holes, leaders and aspirant leaders would do well to fit their personality to the type of organization that best suits their own leadership styles and abilities.

THE GENDER AGENDA

Although the feminist movement can trace a long history, it was not until the late 1980s that a serious study was done into the way women lead. The International Women's Forum asked Judy Rosener at the University of California's Graduate School of Management to research men and women leaders in early 1989. All members of the Forum - founded to enable prominent women leaders around the world to share knowledge - were sent a questionnaire and asked to nominate a man in a similar organization with similar responsibilities. The men were then sent the same questionnaire.

The research showed that, contrary to popular conception, the men and women earned almost exactly the same amount. What Rosener did find, however, was a difference in leadership style.[4] The men tended to describe a "transactional" style, the women a more "transformational" style (see Chapter 8 for more detail). The men used power based on their organizational position and formal authority, while the women ascribed their power to personal characteristics, such as interpersonal skills and hard work, or a network of personal contacts.

Rosener believed that, while the first generation of women who had broken through the "glass ceiling" had done so by following male leadership styles, there was now a second generation finding its own style. "Interactive leadership" was the name Rosener came up with to describe it - reflecting the effort they made to ensure their interactions with subordinates was positive for both sides. Specifically, she found that they encouraged participation, shared power and information, sought to improve people's self-worth, and then got them excited and energized about their work.

One of the conclusions that Rosener reached was that many of the women had simply used behaviors and beliefs that came naturally to them. Starting off in male-dominated organizations, they had lacked formal authority over others, but had found that by using behavior that was natural, or at least socially acceptable to them, they could become leaders. She also highlighted that at a time of rapid change, in a world where young professional workers wanted greater participation, a more interactive style of leadership – as displayed by these women – might be the best approach.

In 1990, the same year that Rosener's research was published, Sally Helgesen's book *The Female Advantage: Women's Ways of Leadership*[5] added considerably to the debate. Helgesen had studied four women leaders and concluded that their strategies represented a highly successful alternative to male leadership styles. She proposed that men and women approach work in fundamentally different ways and that many of these differences give women a distinct advantage over men. Women, she argued, excelled at running organizations that foster creativity, co-operation, and intuitive decision-making power – all necessities for companies of the future.

In line with Rosener's findings, Helgesen suggested that organizations run by women break away from traditional hierarchy, and more closely resemble an inclusive web, where relationships draw people closer around a common purpose and create communities where information sharing is essential (see also Chapter 9).

In 1992, futurologist John Naisbitt co-wrote *Megatrends for Women* with Patricia Aburdene. In it they used the term "women leadership" to describe what they saw as women's values and leadership behaviors. They identified 25 behaviors that characterized women's leadership and clustered them into six fundamental patterns: behaviors that empower, restructure, teach, provide role models, encourage openness, and stimulate questioning.

In 1995, Rosener followed up her earlier work with a book entitled *America's Competitive Secret: Women Managers*. The "secret" was the number of well-educated, experienced professional women ready, willing, and able to take leadership roles in the US – a vast, untapped economic resource. Top women leaders and managers, she argued, cope well with ambiguity, are comfortable sharing power, and they tend to empower others – all leadership qualities increasingly in demand.

The debate about the difference between men and women as leaders, and the natural ability of women to provide the new forms of leadership – suitable for the twenty-first century – has continued for a decade. By and large, studies by academics find little difference between men's and women's leadership styles, their attitudes to leadership, or their leadership behaviors, whereas anecdotal and case study based work highlights the fact that women do tend, apart from other things, to be more people-oriented and less bothered about ego and image.

So, we can be clear that this debate will run and run. Perhaps one of its biggest values has been to keep alive the questioning of old-fashioned views and attitudes about what constitutes an appropriate leadership style. Beyond that, it is perfectly open to any or all of us to use our intuition to acknowledge the likelihood that "feminine" traits such as being understanding, sensitive, compassionate, and intuitive are more appropriate in certain circumstances than "masculine" traits such as being dominant, aggressive, competitive, and analytical. But, as the whole body of thinking on leadership styles has come to recognize since the 1960s, it all depends on the situation. And, as repeated studies show – including Rosener's 1989 work – men can display feminine characteristics and women can adopt masculine ones.

SERVANT LEADERSHIP

Robert Greenleaf spent most of his working life at US telecom giant AT&T, where he became vice-president responsible for management development and education. Once retired, he began a second career as a teacher and consultant at places like Harvard Business School and the Ford Foundation. Perplexed by the scale of young people's revolt in the 1960s, he wrote and published a short essay in 1970 entitled *The Servant as Leader*. In it he argued the case for a leadership style that sought to bring out people's full potential, by listening to their needs and then empowering them to act, a type of leadership that – through an ethic of service – brought out the best in people and society.

He wanted to replace "enforced compliance" with "enthusiastic engagement," and articulated a vision of leadership as something much more than coercive and manipulative power. He argued for a style of leadership designed to make people altogether freer, wiser, and healthier.

At a simplified level, the basic tenets of servant leadership can be defined as:

» recognize other people's unique qualities, treat them as real people. Empathize with them, but don't be condescending;
» listen intently;
» be truly aware – seeing things as they really are, not how you might wish them to be. This goes for self-awareness too;
» involve people directly in building and improving the organization;
» engage people, build consensus, persuade – don't force compliance;
» be intuitive, use your powers of foresight;
» be a visionary, dream dreams;
» see yourself as a steward, leading the organization on trust; and
» develop a deep sense of community among everyone in the organization and work for the greater good of society.

In the hedonistic and materialist world of the 1980s, such sentiments held little appeal outside a relatively limited group of leaders with whom it found immediate personal resonance. One such was Max DePree, CEO and later chairman of the board of Herman Miller Inc., a *Fortune 500* company which consistently appeared in *Fortune*'s list of "Most Admired Companies" (see Chapter 9 for more on DePree's thinking).

By the early 1990s, however, interest was renewed when Larry Spears, the director of the Greenleaf Center, edited a book[6] in 1995 with a foreword by Max DePree. It contained some 25 chapters written by a variety of specialists, best-known of whom was Peter Senge. The author of best-seller *The Fifth Discipline*, Senge said "I believe that [Greenleaf's] essay, 'The Servant as Leader' is the most singular and useful statement on leadership that I have read in the last 20 years . . . For many years, I simply told people not to waste their time reading all the other managerial leadership books. 'If you are really serious about the deeper territory of true leadership,' I would say, 'read Greenleaf.'"

In 1996 a selection of previously unpublished essays by Greenleaf[7] was published, this time with a foreword by Peter Drucker. This was followed rapidly in 1997 by *Insights on Leadership: Service, Stewardship, Spirit, and Servant-Leadership*, with contributions from other leading management thinkers, including James Kouzes, Margaret Wheatley, Ken Blanchard, and Stephen Covey. Momentum was clearly building.

Then, in 1998, *Fortune* magazine began publishing a new list, called "The 100 Best Companies to Work for in America." This was a reflection of the growing emphasis on people as a critical corporate asset and the need to retain the best in what has become known as "the war for talent." What this new list rapidly revealed was that the companies appearing at the top of the list were following a servant leadership culture. For example, in the 2001 list, first place was taken by Container Store, fourth place by Southwest Airlines (see Chapter 7), sixth place by TD Industries, and eighth place by Synovus Financial Corporation. Each of these companies quite specifically adopts a servant leadership style. From a theoretical concept, servant leadership has suddenly been propelled into the media spotlight and can be seen to have accomplished remarkable results.

Given the time lag in the dissemination of management thinking that exists between the US and the rest of the world, it is reasonable to expect the idea of servant leadership to start receiving much more attention in the near future in Europe, Asia, and the rest of the world. Probably the only reason that it hasn't already become more widespread is that the usual agents of dispersion – the management consultants – have little part to play. This is a style of leadership that is highly personal to the individual leader or leaders. It is not a style of leadership that can be learnt (though one can learn about it) nor is it a Band-Aid that can be quickly stuck onto an organization in trouble. But expect to hear more. Possibly a good deal more.

FOUR TRICKS OF THE TRADE

Finally, Robert Goffee and Gareth Jones (see above), who have enjoyed asking leaders and potential leaders the question "why would anyone follow you?", have identified, in an award-winning article, what they believe are essential qualities to persuade people to be followers[8] – four, possibly unexpected, ways of behaving that can win hearts and minds.

Reveal your weakness(es)

In today's business environment pretending to be perfect just isn't credible. We all have strengths and weaknesses and exposing a weakness or two can play a big part in establishing trust. By being vulnerable, leaders can also emphasize their approachability and humanity. As Goffee and Jones point out, exposing some weakness also means that your peers, colleagues, and subordinates don't have to invent one for you!

But it has to be done carefully. Leaders should choose which weaknesses to expose and, whatever happens, never reveal what might be seen as a fatal flaw. The weakness(es) should be peripheral – for instance, Richard Branson of Virgin always looks slightly ill-at-ease and fumbles when interviewed in public, it is part of his appeal. See also the section on Herb Kelleher's smoking and drinking in Chapter 7. Or the weakness can be one that in some lights may be seen as a strength – for instance, being a workaholic. But, whatever happens, don't invent a weakness – that creates double incredibility.

Be different

Goffee and Jones believe that the most important quality is to acknowledge, understand, and play up our individual unique differences. This may be our physical appearance or our style of dress – John Harvey-Jones, former CEO of ICI, played up his moustache, his long hair, and his loud ties. It made him stand out. (Again, see the section on Herb Kelleher in Chapter 7.)

But there are many other differences – the way we use our voice, display our emotions, how we greet people, even how we walk. Used carefully, such differences can produce separateness, and Goffee and Jones emphasize that for leaders this is important. Achieving the right social distance is, in their view, a vital part of being a leader: "leadership, after all, is not a popularity contest."

Use your instincts and intuition

Good leaders use their instinct and intuition to know how and when to reveal a weakness or highlight a difference – one draws people closer, the other creates a distance. They also use their senses to choose a course of action and gauge the right timing. This means picking up "weak" signals around them – feeling shifts in opinion, climate, and ambience, and reading subtle, often non-verbal, clues.

There is an inevitable downside. Judgments are often fine and it is easy to get it wrong and overstep the mark. Bob Horton, CEO of BP in the early 1990s, marked his own difference by displaying his powerful intellect – but he failed to recognize that people saw him as arrogant and self-important (see section on David Simon in Chapter 7).

Sensing is much more than simply double-guessing; it involves listening, feeling, and learning from experience. It means being able to separate background "noise" and personal "projection" from the reality of the situation.

Be empathetic but tough

Leaders need to blend these qualities – humanity and approachability; separateness and difference; intuition and instinct – into their leadership style. It is easy in today's democratic styles of management to be drawn into an excessive emphasis on employees' feelings and concerns. Goffee and Jones argue that this can threaten good leadership. Of course it is critical to convince them that you care, but that must not disadvantage the job to be done. The skill is to combine the two – genuinely care about employees but really push them too (see section on Konosuke Matsushita in Chapter 7). The message is then clear: both people *and* the job matter! People commit to leaders who push them to achieve, more than they do to those who are just trying to be nice.

KEY LEARNING POINTS

Some different issues in the leadership styles debate:

» 1990s research suggests that CEOs have just five basic leadership styles, they overlap, but not by much – Bain.
» Situations matter, none more so than the stage of an organization's development. Effective leadership styles differ at each stage – Schein and others.
» Organizations differ and so do the leadership requirements needed by each type – Goffee and Jones.
» A good deal of research suggests that women have a different leadership style to men, one that is seen as much more appropriate for today's business and organizational environment than the typically male approach – Rosener, Helgesen.

» Servant leadership is rapidly growing as an area of interest, research, and corporate commitment – Greenleaf and others.
» When it comes down to style, there are some tricks of the trade that seem to work – Goffee and Jones.

NOTES

1 Edgar Schein, "Leadership and Organizational Culture," in *The Leader of the Future*, Jossey-Bass, 1996.
2 C. Clarke and S. Pratt, "Leadership's four part progress," *Management Today*, 1985.
3 Robert Goffee and Gareth Jones, *The Character of a Corporation: How your company's culture can make or break your business*, HarperBusiness, 1998.
4 Judy Rosener, "Ways Women Lead," *Harvard Business Review*, November–December, 1990.
5 Sally Helgesen, *The Female Advantage: Women's Ways of Leadership*, Currency/Doubleday, 1995.
6 Larry Spears (ed.), *et al.*, *Reflections on Leadership: How Robert K. Greenleaf's Theory of Servant-Leadership Influenced Today's Top Management Thinkers*, John Wiley & Sons, May, 1995.
7 Larry Spears, *et al.*, *On Becoming a Servant-Leader*, Jossey-Bass, 1996.
8 Robert Goffee and Gareth Jones, "Why should anyone be led by you?", *Harvard Business Review*, September–October, 2000.

In Practice – Successful Leadership Styles

What makes for effective leadership style? Chapter 7 looks at three very different forms of successful leadership style. It explains and draws lessons from:

» David Simon of BP – the diplomatic transformer;
» Konosuke Matsushita of Matsushita Electric – the leader-philosopher; and
» Herb Kelleher of Southwest Airlines – the servant leader.

"People with different personalities, different approaches, different values succeed not because one set of values or practices is superior, but because their values and practices are genuine."

Herb Kelleher, CEO Southwest Airlines

DAVID SIMON – THE DIPLOMATIC TRANSFORMER

BP's origins date back to 1901, when William Knox D'Arcy, who had made a fortune from mining in Australia, negotiated a concession with the grand vizier of Persia to look for oil. Seven years later his company became the first to strike oil in the Middle East. Keen to secure essential wartime supplies, the British Navy persuaded the UK government to buy a majority stake in the company in 1914. This remained the case until 1977, when Labour prime minister Jim Callaghan began a privatization process by selling a tranche of the government's shares. The process was completed in October 1987 when Margaret Thatcher's Conservative government sold its remaining 31.5% holding.

Although it was a cumbersome, sprawling company, BP was the first to find gas in the UK sector of the North Sea in 1965, and the first to bring North Sea oil ashore from its Forties field a few years later. In 1968, after 10 years of exploration, BP had also discovered oil at Prudhoe Bay in Alaska, part of a vast new oilfield. As a result the company was able to weather the storms of the oil crises of the 1970s.

BP America

In order to develop Prudhoe Bay, BP had invested in Standard Oil of Cleveland, Ohio (Sohio). In 1987 it bought the remaining 45% it didn't already own and, merging its other US activities, formed BP America. Robert Horton, who had worked at BP for 30 years including time as CEO of BP Chemicals and as main board finance director, was made CEO of the new operation. His reputation as "Horton the Hatchet" – for demanding job cuts to stem losses – preceded him.[1]

In fact Horton, who had taken an MBA at MIT's Sloan School of Management in the 1970s, liked Americans and worked hard to assimilate their culture. Though it was inevitable that jobs would have to go, he talked straight and persuaded people that he was rebuilding the business, not destroying it. He took Jack Welch, GE's blunt and forthright CEO, as a role model, cutting out layers, but holding "town meetings" at BP offices across the US to explain his strategy (see Chapter 7 in *Leadership Express* in the *ExpressExec* series). He joined in the Republican presidential campaign in 1988, contemplated running for the US Senate himself, and made a good impression on the Cleveland social circuit.

New ideas, new style

Marked out as the heir apparent to succeed Sir Peter Walters as BP's CEO, Horton planned to bring what he had found great about America back to Britain. The *Wall Street Journal*, applauding Horton as "an unusually brash Briton enamored of the US," wrote in 1989 that he wanted to "Americanize Britain's biggest company." Horton underlined this by expressing the belief that "BP is, in a funny sense, more of an American company than a British company."[2]

On his formal appointment as chairman and CEO in September 1989, Horton set about changing BP with vigor. He announced that the company would have to undergo "the corporate equivalent of *Perestroika* and *Glasnost*."[3] Widely welcomed in the media and among financial analysts as someone who could cut through BP's stifling bureaucracy and over-centralized systems, Horton launched "Project 1990" to change the "civil service" culture that still reflected the company's previous government ownership. He also wanted to flatten the organization, make deep cuts in head-office functions, and decentralize power to global business streams. The process changes Horton envisaged were encapsulated in the slogan "OPEN" – Open thinking, Personal impact, Empowering, and Networking – networked, empowered teams were to be the change-management tool.

Mismatch

Initially, all went well, with senior executives such as David Simon, BP's chief operating officer, supporting the much-needed changes. However, many people became unhappy with the way change was being imposed – Horton used words like "trust" and "empowerment," but showed little sign of it in the way he was pushing the changes through. His assertive American leadership style began to get in the way of what he was trying to achieve.

By 1992, as the economic recession continued, BP's financial situation worsened dramatically and Horton implemented swingeing cost cuts. Head office staff was cut from 3000 in 1989 to just 380. Morale plummeted as many saw his change program increasingly indistinguishable from a large-scale downsizing exercise. Horton then exacerbated things by adopting an ever more dismissive tone about his colleagues. In an interview with *Forbes* magazine in the US he said: "Because I am blessed with my good brain, I tend to get to the right answer rather quicker and more often than most people... So I have to rein in my impatience."[4]

Widespread unease turned to real concern about Horton's judgment and leadership style. In June, 1992 the company's non-executive directors acted, informing Horton that he would have to go. On 25 June, he resigned after little more than two years in the job. David Simon was asked to take over.

New leader, different style

Simon had to move fast on several fronts. The business was burdened with debt and was heading for its first loss in 80 years – so major change would have to continue. But shattered morale and widespread distrust would have to be repaired simultaneously.

On the financial front, Simon developed a three-year plan, called "1-2-5" – to cut debt by $1bn a year, build profits to $2bn a year, and hold capital spending to $5bn a year. With a much smaller head office staff, he sold BP's headquarters and disposed of $6bn of non-core businesses. He speeded reorganization by pushing decision making down the company and changed the management structure so that managers could co-operate across divisions rather than referring everything upwards for decisions. As far as continuing change was concerned, Simon launched a new program called "PRT" – Performance, Reputation, and Teams – which, despite the name change, was fundamentally a reshaped version of Horton's OPEN.

By setting specific targets and focusing everyone on them, Simon gave BP's people clear reasons why they would have to become cost-conscious and help the company back to profitability. By constantly communicating, he regained their trust in senior management. He made no bones about the scale of change that was needed and declared early on that he would be continuing Horton's strategy: "This is about the style of running the company at the top." He told the *Financial Times*: "It is not about changes in strategy."[5] But, where Horton had been blunt and abrasive, Simon was calm and diplomatic – though anyone who mistook his mild manner for weakness was in for a surprise.

With a firm grip on the numbers he wanted, Simon helped people work out how to achieve them. He made it clear that he wanted to listen, to think through problems without jumping to conclusions, and liked to provide space for other people's ideas. He thus made clear his own personal commitment to teamwork. He also made himself approachable – often wandering around talking to secretaries, tea ladies, and anyone he met. By acting in these ways, Simon not only won trust and confidence, he also personally engendered a new, freer, more democratic and empowering way of working. But throughout he never took his eye off what the business had to achieve.

The achievement

By late 1994, most of his three-year plan had been achieved – a year early. In 1995, Simon moved up to become chairman and brought in John Browne, previously head of BP's exploration division, as his CEO. By the following year, BP's share price had doubled compared with 1992 and even though the company's workforce had fallen from 117,000 to 56,000, morale and confidence were high.

When he left BP to take up a political appointment with the new Labour government in 1997, Simon bequeathed Browne a company in such good condition that in 1998 it could pay $48bn for US oil major Amoco. The following year BP Amoco announced that it was acquiring Atlantic Richfield for $26.8bn. The turnaround since the low spot of 1992 had been dramatic.

INSIGHTS INTO LEADERSHIP STYLES – ROBERT HORTON AND DAVID SIMON

» There are few such clear examples of differing leadership styles and their relative effects. CEOs are usually removed because of strategic error or failure to achieve expected financial targets.

Very few indeed are expelled for an inappropriate leadership style – especially over such a short period.

» Few doubted Horton's intellectual ability, nor the strategy he chose to follow. But, having assimilated an American style of leadership he showed a blind spot in applying it in an unadulterated form in the company's UK operations. What works in one situation may not work in another.

» David Simon, who had initially been passed over in favor of Horton because the latter was seen to have a proven leadership track record, used a style that matched the situation. He pursued the same strategy and changes, but simply did it differently. By personifying the behaviors he wanted to embed, rather than telling people how to behave, he achieved the critical goals.

» Simon mixed "hardware" with "software." He blended a focus on what had to be achieved with sensitivity to the situation, approachability, and good communication skills. He won trust, respect, and confidence.

BP time-line

» **1986**: Robert Horton appointed CEO of Sohio.

» **1987**: British government sells remaining shares in BP, completing its privatization.

» **1987**: BP completes acquisition of Sohio and Robert Horton appointed CEO of BP America.

» **1989**: BP starts sale of non-core assets and Robert Horton appointed to succeed Sir Peter Walters as BP's chairman and CEO.

» **1990**: Project 1990 and OPEN launched.

» **1992**: Robert Horton resigns and David Simon takes over. Company announces first loss in 80 years.

» **1994**: Simon's three-year plan achieved one year early.

» **1995**: Simon becomes chairman, John Browne appointed CEO.

» **1996**: Share price double that at the 1992 low point.

» **1998**: Amoco offers itself for sale to BP.

» **1999**: BP Amoco acquires Atlantic Richfield.

KONOSUKE MATSUSHITA – THE LEADER PHILOSOPHER

Konosuke Matsushita was born in a rural Japanese village in 1894, the youngest of eight children. After his father lost their home and farmland through speculating in rice, the family moved to the city of Wakayama when Konosuke was only five. After another business failure, his father moved to Osaka where he told his youngest son to join him. Aged nine, and without finishing primary school, Konosuke began working a 16-hour day as an apprentice with a local charcoal brazier. A year later he was working in a bicycle shop. When he was 16, he found work with Osaka Electric Light Company, where he was rapidly promoted and continued to work for eight years.

Then, at the age of 22, Matsushita took an unusual step. He had begun to suffer respiratory problems and lost pay for the frequent days he had to take off. He also found his work boring. So he decided to start working for himself, making a Y-shaped adapter he had invented that allowed both a bulb and an electrical appliance to be plugged into the same light socket.

Entrepreneur

His wife, his brother-in-law, and two colleagues from his old company joined him. Unfortunately, the adaptor did not sell and Matsushita had to pawn his wife's kimonos to find working capital. His two former colleagues soon left, but the little business was saved by an order for insulator plates for electric fans from a nearby electrical company and, in 1918, the Matsushita Electric Appliance Factory was established. Within a year it was employing 20 people.

Five years later, Matsushita launched an innovative product, a bullet-shaped, battery-powered bicycle lamp. Unfortunately, it also did not sell well – most people were happy with the candle or paraffin lamps they were already using. Determined not to be beaten, Matsushita ensured that every bicycle retailer in Osaka was visited. Each was left with one of his torches, switched on. As people realized they ran for 30 or 40 hours, sales picked up rapidly and soon the business was able to begin developing a national network of sales agents. Within two years, the company had introduced "National" as its first trademark and, by diversifying into electric irons, radios, and other allied products, was becoming a significant business in Japan's wholesale and retail markets. His business was prospering.

Caring for people

As in many parts of the world during the 1920s, labor unrest was common in Japan. Matsushita had always treated his employees as part of a family, but responded to this intensifying activity by introducing a series of innovations that were well ahead of their time. In the mid-1920s, he formed a club called Hoichi Kai, designed to look after employees' health and foster good relations through social benefits, sports days, and cultural festivals. Its slogan was "we all walk together one step at a time." In another imaginative move, Matsushita introduced an in-house magazine to improve communications in 1927.

In 1929 he went a step further. Using the slogan "harmony between corporate profit and social justice," he launched a company creed: "Recognizing our responsibilities as industrialists, we will devote ourselves to the progress and development of society and the well-being of people, thereby enhancing the quality of life throughout the world." With this creed came a pledge that he asked all employees to make: "We pledge to work together, in the spirit of mutual trust and through selfless devotion to our jobs, to achieve a continuous improvement of our corporate and personal performance."

The Depression

These fine words were soon to be severely tested. In the following year the Great Depression hit Japan and within a short time, Matsushita Electric's sales had halved. Across the country, companies were slashing their workforce and Matsushita's colleagues proposed that their own should be halved. But Matsushita ordered that no employee be laid off. Instead he halved working hours, which reduced production by 50%, but continued to pay everyone their normal wages. Matsushita's workforce responded. By using their spare time and weekends to sell the company's products personally, they cleared the company's backlog of stock within two months.

Matsushita's action stood in stark contrast to other Japanese firms and because it was successful in both the short and long term – morale, motivation, and productivity all grew and stayed high – he is seen as the person who pioneered Japan's longstanding commitment between employer and employee.

Leadership philosophy

At around this time, Matsushita visited the head temple of the Tenrikyo religious sect, where he saw people working hard but happily together without any pay. He came away with a feeling that if only a business could somehow be made meaningful – like a religion – people would be both more satisfied and more productive.[6] He began searching for a philosophy that would encompass his care and respect for people and the role of a business.

Having devoted a lot of thought to it, in 1932, to mark the business' fifteenth anniversary, he called a meeting of senior managers to announce the company's purpose. "The mission of a manufacturer is to overcome poverty, to relieve society as a whole from the misery of poverty and bring it wealth. Business and production are not meant to enrich only the shops or the factories of the enterprise concerned, but all the rest of society as well. And society needs the dynamism and vitality of business and industry to generate its wealth. Only under such conditions will businesses and factories truly prosper, but their prosperity is secondary. Our primary concern is to eliminate poverty and increase wealth by producing goods in abundant supply... This is a manufacturer's true mission." Matsushita had found a vision and higher-level purpose that went well beyond the simple pursuit of profit.

A year later, in 1933, he went further still, issuing what were to become his and his company's guiding principles right up to the present day:

» service to the public – by providing high-quality goods and services at reasonable prices, we contribute to the public's well-being;
» fairness and honesty – we will be fair and honest in all our business dealings and personal conduct;
» teamwork for the common cause – we will pool our abilities, based on mutual trust and respect;
» untiring effort for improvement – we will constantly strive to improve our corporate and personal performances;

» courtesy and humility – we will always be cordial and modest and respect the rights and needs of others;

» accordance with natural laws – we will abide by the laws of nature and adjust to the ever-changing conditions around us; and

» gratitude for blessings – we will always be grateful for all the blessings and kindness we have received.

These principles were remarkable for their time. To inspire his employees to share his philosophy and vision he insisted, despite some opposition, that all employees should repeat them aloud each day before work began – a practice subsequently followed by many other Japanese companies. These "Seven Spirits of Matsushita," as they are known today, were to find constant expression in Matsushita's own leadership style. He believed in the potential that every human being possessed, and saw a successful business as the way to help as many people as possible to fulfil that potential. To be successful needed hard work and commitment, but it had to work both ways. He was a competitive and demanding entrepreneur who believed that personal humility and respect for other people was the right way of winning that commitment.

Renewed growth

The Japanese economy began to recover strongly in 1932 and, by the time Matsushita Electric became an incorporated company in 1935, it had nearly 5000 employees. Still suffering from ill health, Matsushita decided to delegate more responsibilities. To do so, he divisionalized the company – thus making it one of the first companies in the world to adopt this structure. The business prospered. But Japan was soon to enter World War II, and under orders from the militarist government Matsushita Electric soon found itself required to work with large industrial combines – the *zaibatsu* – to help make aircraft and ships.

The War's aftermath

The defeat of Japan in 1945, and the bombing that preceded it, left the country completely devastated. Determined to ensure that "a former enemy would never again become a threat to world peace," the US occupation force began the systematic disbandment of Japan's military structure and its industrial *zaibatsu*. Because Matsushita Electric had worked with these combines, Matsushita and his family were designated as a " *zaibatsu* family" and the company was declared a " *zaibatsu* company."

Despite a petition signed by 15,000 of Matsushita Electric's employees, and representations by their trade unions, Matsushita was thus personally barred from holding an executive position at his company. However, with hyper-inflation, severe food shortages, and desperately low morale all around, Matsushita founded and then devoted his energies to the PHP Institute – standing for "Peace and Happiness through Prosperity" – in November 1946. The following year the exclusion order on Matsushita was lifted and both founder and company were reunited.

Matsushita reintroduced all the policies and principles that he had developed before the war and which had subsequently fallen into disuse. As a result, the company quickly started to thrive again. During the 1950s, the company launched washing machines, black-and-white television sets, and refrigerators. In the 1960s, it launched tape recorders, color televisions, microwave ovens, and the first video-tape recorders. Significantly, in 1960, just a year before Matsushita relinquished the role of president and became chairman, Matsushita Electric became the first Japanese company to introduce a five-day working week.

As chairman, Matsushita turned to writing – producing 44 books, many directed toward the future of Japanese society and the world – one of which sold over 4 million copies.[7] Between 1963 and 1988 he personally donated billions of Yen to many educational institutions in Japan and abroad. Throughout, he tirelessly propounded his personal philosophy, as encapsulated in a short piece of his writing:

"'The Untrapped Mind'
The 'untrapped mind' is open enough to see many possibilities, humble enough to learn from anyone and anything, forbearing

enough to forgive all, perceptive enough to see things as they really are, and reasonable enough to judge their true value."

The achievement

Konosuke Matsushita died of pneumonia on April 27, 1989. He was 94 years old. In his lifetime he became one of the world's pre-eminent industrialists, building the business that bears his name into the world's largest consumer electronics company, with familiar brands such as Panasonic, Technics, National, and Quasar. Today, it has over 40,000 employees in more than 200 companies in 46 countries. Its turnover in 2000 was just over $70bn.[8]

Known as the "god of management" in Japan, Matsushita's innovations in the 1930s – for instance, teamwork, continuous improvement, customer first – are still being adopted elsewhere. His genuine concern for people, his respect for others and his personal humility has made him a powerful role model.

This is exemplified by a simple story from the time when Matsushita was at the height of his renown across Japan. He went for lunch with some colleagues to a local Osaka restaurant. Upon his arrival, everyone eating there recognized the great man and stopped to bow and acknowledge his presence. Matsushita honored the welcome and took his seat. At the end of the meal, with half of his food unfinished, Matsushita asked the manager if he could go through to the kitchen and speak to the chef. The manager immediately demurred and instead brought the quaking chef out into the restaurant. Matsushita explained: "I felt that if you saw I had only eaten half of my meal, you would think that I did not like the food, or did not care for how you prepared it. I want you to know that the food and your preparation of it was excellent. It is one of the best meals I have had. I am just old now and cannot eat as much as I used to. I wanted you to know that and to thank you personally." Thus did Matsushita live the beliefs he espoused.

Although Matsushita's philosophy predated the servant leadership style first promulgated by Greenleaf in 1970 (see Chapter 6), it is remarkably similar – he saw himself as an industrialist whose role was to serve others and, by empowering them, to allow them to achieve their full potential.

INSIGHTS INTO LEADERSHIP STYLES – KONOSUKE MATSUSHITA

» Coming from an affluent family that had fallen on hard times, Matsushita understood what hard work and poverty meant. Once his own business began to flourish, he did not forget those early lessons but sought to find ways to improve the lot of his employees, and many others, by the way he ran the business.

» He believed there was more to running a business than making profits – though he never doubted the importance of being profitable. By seeking a wider purpose and value he established principles based on a vision that won commitment.

» By establishing those principles and sticking to them, Matsushita established a style of leadership that was emulated throughout Japan. From the 1980s onward, many concepts were widely adopted in the West. The fact that he is much less well-known outside Japan is a reflection of his humility – he did not seek publicity unless it was in a good cause.

Matsushita Electric time-line

» **1894**: Konosuke Matsushita born.
» **1917**: Matsushita starts own small business.
» **1918**: Matsushita Electric established.
» **1923**: Bullet-shaped bicycle lamp manufactured and marketed.
» **1929**: Company creed and pledge announced.
» **1930**: All employees retained and kept on full pay during Great Depression.
» **1932**: Company mission and guiding principles announced.
» **1933**: Company divisionalized.
» **1935**: Matsushita Electric Industrial Co Ltd incorporated; 5,000 employees.
» **1941**: Japan enters World War II.
» **1946**: Matsushita and his company designated *zaibatsu*.
» **1946**: Matsushita starts PHP to promote peacetime industry.
» **1947**: Matsushita declassified as *zaibatsu*.
» **1950s**: Company expands rapidly.

» **1960s**: Company expands into electronics and goes multinational.
» **1961**: Matsushita resigns as president and becomes chairman.
» **1989**: Matsushita dies, aged 94.

HERB KELLEHER – A SERVANT LEADER

A lawyer by profession, Herb Kelleher was working at a San Antonio law firm in 1966 when he went out for lunch with one of his clients, a Texas businessman called Rollin King who had run a small air taxi service. Over a drink King picked up a napkin and drew a triangle on it, writing Dallas, Houston, and San Antonio at the three corners. King was suggesting that they start a new Texas-based airline together. Legend has it that Kelleher briefly shut his eyes, paused and then said ''Rollin, you are crazy . . . But let's do it!'' Kelleher agreed to put up a $10,000 stake and the business that was to become Southwest Airlines had been born.

At the time, air travel was still relatively exclusive, with only 20% of US citizens having ever traveled by commercial airline. Kelleher and King's concept was for a no-frills, low fare, short-haul, point-to-point airline that could capitalize on the booming Texan economy. It was thus a direct challenge to the established airlines.

So, as soon as it applied for a license in 1967, Southwest immediately became entangled in legal battles with Braniff, Texas International and Continental, who all contended that the Texas skies were already too crowded for yet another airline. Kelleher argued the case all the way up to the US Supreme Court and won. But it took three-and-a-half years and when they finally got permission to operate, in 1971, the company's finances were in a dire state, with $183 in the bank and debts of $80,000.

Take off

Nevertheless, with the help of Lamar Muse, a man with years of experience at senior level in the airline industry, who had been appointed president of Southwest in January 1971, the airline began service on June 18, 1971. To mark out its difference, cabin staff wore extremely short hot pants in bright orange, knee-high white PVC go-go-girl boots, and wide belts that emphasized shapely bodies. Targeting businessmen, the airline promised them "love" – using the slogan "Somebody up there loves you." Flying from Dallas' Love Field airport, the drinks on board were called "love potions" and the peanuts the staff served were called "love bites."

Harried by the big airlines, who used their financial muscle to try to squeeze them out of business, Southwest lost over $3mn in its first year. But a remarkable fighting spirit and *esprit de corps* had developed among the 200 or so employees – for example, finding ways to cut airport turnaround time from 45 to 15 minutes. By 1973, the company was in profit. In 1974, it carried its millionth passenger. In 1977, the company's stock was listed on the New York Stock Exchange with the three-letter designation "LUV."

Change at the top

Then, in 1978, a growing rift between Lamar Muse and Rollin King came to a head and the board asked Herb Kelleher to take over as president, CEO, and chairman. Up until then Kelleher had been working with his law firm and had not been deeply involved in running the business, so he only accepted the posts on an interim basis. But when a new CEO was appointed later in the year, Kelleher stayed on as chairman and from then on he became more and more caught up in Southwest, finally taking over as president, chairman, and CEO in 1982.

When he took over, the airline had just 27 planes, $270mn in revenues, 2100 employees, and flew to 14 cities. For the next 23 years his personality and leadership would play the dominant part in the company's growing success. When he retired in June, 2001, it had over 350 planes, revenues of $5.7bn, more than 30,000 employees, and flew to 57 cities. Its market capitalization, at $14bn, was bigger than the combined capitalizations of American Airlines, United Airlines, and Houston-based Continental Airline's.

A chain-smoker, with a gravelly voice and a well-publicized fondness for Wild Turkey bourbon whiskey, Kelleher had used the four years from 1978 to 1982 to understand what had made the company successful, and he now set about embedding it in everything the business did. In the process he made his own idiosyncratic leadership style an integral part of the company's public profile – internally and externally.

People

He recognized that the high level of customer service that Southwest offered was a direct result of the attitudes of its employees. So, contrary to conventional wisdom, he made employees – not customers or shareholders – the number one priority. "Your employees come first. There's no question about that. And if your employees are satisfied and happy and dedicated and inspired by what they're doing, then they make your customers happy and they come back and that makes your shareholders happy."[9]

Customer service required going the extra mile and so employing the right people became the top priority. Fundamental to Southwest's recruitment philosophy is a motto: "hire for attitude, train for skill." To provide Southwest's "Positively Outrageous Service" requires an ability to be nonconformist. For example, one recruitment advertisement showed a picture of a dinosaur that had been enthusiastically colored in by an elementary-school child. Attached is a note from his teacher: "Brian – please try to color inside the lines!" The advertisement's headline reads "Brian Shows an Early Aptitude for Working at Southwest Airlines."[10] It is not unknown for 100 people to be interviewed for a relatively simple job like ramp attendant.

Empowerment

Kelleher believes people should be themselves at work, not try to fit into a predefined mold: "they can behave the way that their basic natures influence them to behave. If they want to tell jokes, they can tell jokes. If they want to play practical jokes, they can play practical jokes, and they can, in effect, be a liberated spirit within a working environment."

"Do what you think is right" is Kelleher's constant message to staff. This means looking for a lost teddy bear, parking a customer's car when they're running late, using their own credit card if someone's lost their purse. "If you exercise this form of leadership, we've learned that people become healthier, wiser, freer, and more human."[11]

Fun, freedom

Fun and freedom are part of the Southwest culture. Anniversaries, birthdays, personal successes, and other celebrations are reasons for a party or picnic and everyone joins in. Kelleher is often involved and, when it was pointed out to him that mechanics on the night shift found it difficult to participate in company picnics, he and some pilots cooked a barbecue for them at two o'clock in the morning. He arrives unannounced with coffee and doughnuts for the cleaning crews at three o'clock.

The informality and fun at Southwest is legendary. As part of safety instructions, cabin crew have been known to say: "There may be fifty ways to leave your lover, but there are only six ways to leave this aircraft." People calling Southwest's reservations line are quite likely to hear: "If you've been waiting more than 10 seconds, press 8. It won't help, but it might make you feel better."

Being different

Kelleher has made his drinking and smoking a trademark. If he gives a speech at a working breakfast, he points out that it's a unique experience because he seldom speaks when he's sober, and the downside is that he'll remember what he's said. He smokes constantly and nobody is surprised that he keeps a dispenser filled with his favorite Wild Turkey in one of Southwest's conference rooms.

He arrives at company gatherings on a Harley-Davidson motorcycle in jeans and a T-shirt. He sings rap songs with lyrics that make fun of himself. To celebrate the company's 25th anniversary, he was escorted to the podium in a straitjacket. One of his most publicity-conscious moments was in 1992 when he agreed to arm-wrestle the chairman of another company, in a downtown Dallas club, over the right to use the slogan "Just Plane Smart."

For the match, which was later shown on prime-time television, Kelleher wore a white T-shirt, gray tracksuit bottoms under shiny red boxing shorts, with a sling on his right arm and smoked a cigarette. He was accompanied by an assistant wearing a bandoleer filled with rows of airline-sized bottles of Wild Turkey whiskey. When he lost, Kelleher blamed his defeat on a hairline wrist fracture, a week-long cold, a stubborn case of athlete's foot, and having accidentally over-trained by walking up a flight of stairs.

Servant leadership

But these activities hide a deeper sense of leadership. "I have always believed that the best leader is the best server," says Kelleher. "And if you're a servant, by definition, you're not controlling. We try to value each person individually and to be cognizant of them as human beings – not just people who work for our company."[12]

"We are not looking for blind obedience. We are looking for people who, on their own initiative, want to be doing what they are doing because they consider it a worthy objective. I have always believed that the best leader is the best server." For Herb Kelleher, "leadership is being a faithful, devoted, hard-working servant of the people you lead and participating with them in the agonies as well as the ecstasies of life."[13]

Humility

For Kelleher, servant leadership is something else as well: "First of all, it's an attitude of humility, one of modesty."[14] His own office is simple, with an inexpensive desk and a plain oak bookshelf that houses models of Harley-Davidson motorcycles and a bottle of Wild Turkey bourbon.

Kelleher takes little credit for the company's good fortune and consistently deflects praise to his employees. His testimony to the US National Civil Aviation Review Commission is typical: "My name is Herb Kelleher. I co-founded Southwest Airlines in 1967. Because I am unable to perform competently any meaningful function at Southwest, our 25,000 employees let me be CEO. That is one among many reasons why I love the people of Southwest Airlines."

Achievements

Apart from the financial success of Southwest – it is the only US airline to have earned a profit every year since 1973 – the company has been voted one of "The 50 Most Coveted Employers" by MBA students, is ranked fourth by *Fortune* as the company of choice to work for, and was voted the most admired airline in the world for four consecutive years, 1997–2000.

In May 1988, Southwest was the first airline to win the US Department of Transportation's coveted Triple Crown for Best On-time Record, Best Baggage Handling, and Fewest Customer Complaints. Since then they've won the monthly award more than 30 times. Between 1992 and 1995, the company also won the annual award for four consecutive years. In 1996, Kelleher challenged his employees to make it five in a row. They responded with a "Gimme 5" campaign that won the title again in 1996.

One of Kelleher's biggest achievements is his relationship with his staff. This is best reflected in an advertisement they placed in *USA Today* on October 14, 1994 – "Bosses Day" in the US. Costing $60,000, and paid for out of their own pockets, the copy of the advertisement, addressed to Kelleher, read: "For remembering every one of our names. For supporting Ronald McDonald house [Southwest's official charity]. For helping load baggage on Thanksgiving. For giving everyone a kiss (and we mean everyone). For listening. For running the only profitable airline. For singing at our holiday party. For singing only once a year. For letting us wear shorts and sneakers to work. For golfing at the LUV Classic with only one club. For out-talking Sam Donaldson. For riding your Harley-Davidson into Southwest Headquarters. For being a friend, not just a boss." It was signed, "HAPPY BOSSES DAY FROM EACH ONE OF YOUR 16,000 EMPLOYEES."

INSIGHTS INTO LEADERSHIP STYLES – HERB KELLEHER

» Although Kelleher was a founder of Southwest, and sat on its board, he did not become involved in its day-to-day running until 1978 and didn't become full time CEO until 11 years after it began operations. So he adopted a "builder" role (see "Styles for stages" in Chapter 6) – taking the best of the culture and embedding it.

» To provide real customer service – the key to differentiation and therefore profitability – Kelleher recognized that it was employees that mattered most. Finding people with the right attitude became the top priority. Having found the right people, Kelleher then empowered them to make the service special – he did not rely on scripts, procedures, or company policy.

» An intrinsic part of Kelleher's leadership style is "being different," but also being himself. His drinking and smoking are personal habits that he has made a trademark. His Harley-Davidson, T-shirts, and rap songs are unusual CEO behavior. But his people know he cares. (See "Four tricks of the trade" in Chapter 6.)

» Despite being highly successful, Kelleher is modest and humble about his own role (see "Leadership with humility" in Chapter 6 in *Leadership Express* in the *ExpressExec* series). He is a self-proclaimed "servant leader."

Southwest Airlines time-line

» **1966**: Rollin King and Herb Kelleher agree to form intrastate airline.
» **1967**: Court cases to stop airline being licensed begin.
» **1971**: First flight piloted by Lamar Muse.
» **1973**: First profitable year.
» **1974:** Millionth passenger flown.
» **1977**: Five-millionth passenger flown and company listed as LUV on NYSE.
» **1978**: Lamar Muse resigns and Kelleher takes interim charge.
» **1982**: Kelleher becomes president and CEO full-time.
» **1987**: Southwest celebrates the sixth year in a row as recipient of the Best Consumer Satisfaction record of any continental US carrier.
» **1988**: Southwest becomes first airline to win Triple Crown.
» **1990**: Annual revenues more than $1bn – rated a "major" airline.
» **1992**: Kelleher arm-wrestles for right to "Just Plane Smart" slogan, but loses.
» **1992–96**: Southwest wins Triple Crown five years in a row.
» **2001**: Kelleher retires.

NOTES

1 Manfred Kets de Vries, *The New Global Leaders*, Jossey-Bass, 1999.
2 J. Lublin, "Who's News? Horton Seeks an American Accent for BP," *Wall Street Journal*, February 14, 1989.
3 Ian Hargreaves, "When toughness is not enough: the background to the resignation of Bob Horton," *Financial Times*, June 26, 1992.
4 T. Mack, "Eager Lions and Reluctant Lions", *Forbes,* February 17, 1992.

5 David Lascelles, "Horton is ousted as chairman of British Petroleum: directors point to personality clashes as reason for shock decision," *Financial Times*, June 26, 1992.

6 John Kotter, *Matsushita Leadership: Lessons from the 20th Century's most Remarkable Entrepreneur*, Free Press, 1997.

7 Konosuke Matsushita, *Michio Hiraku: Developing a Road to Peace and Happiness through Prosperity*, PHP, 1968.

8 $73bn as of March 12, 2001.

9 *Chief Executive* magazine: http://www.chiefexecutive.net/mag/146/x2article1.htm.

10 Kevin & Jackie Freiberg, *Nuts!: Southwest Airlines' Crazy Recipe for Business and Personal Success*, Bard Press, 1996.

11 *Seen Magazine*: http://www.seen.com/seen_magazine/july2001/fortune.htm.

12 http://www.greenleaf.org/leadership/read-about-it/articles/The-Essentials-of-Servant-Leadership–principles-in-Practice.htm.

13 Kevin & Jackie Freiberg, *Nuts!: Southwest Airlines' Crazy Recipe for Business and Personal Success*, Bard Press, 1996.

14 *Chief Executive* magazine: http://www.chiefexecutive.net/mag/146/article1.htm.

Key Concepts and Thinkers

To understand many of the ideas about leadership style, it's important to know some of the underlying research and concepts. Chapter 8 includes:

» a glossary;
» seven key concepts;
» the difference between transactional and transformational leadership; and
» a brief description of action-centered leadership.

"Often the most important acts of executive leadership is the ability to ask a question that hasn't been asked before, the ability to inquire, not just dictate or advocate. Unfortunately, most people in executive leadership positions are great at advocacy but poor at inquiry."

Peter Senge, author of The Fifth Discipline

Underlying many of the current ideas about leadership styles are some key concepts developed since 1945, when researchers began trying to define what were the most effective ways of leading. What follows is a short glossary and brief definitions of some of the main concepts developed by a variety of key thinkers. Many overlap.

GLOSSARY

Action-centered leadership – See "Key concepts" below.

Charismatic leadership – Leadership based on the charismatic appeal of the leader. See also Chapter 6 in *Leadership Express* in the *ExpressExec* series.

Command and control – An unsophisticated management style in which subordinates are told what to do and have little say in what, why, and when.

Conflict management – Identifying and taking steps to prevent potentially confrontational situations; the management and resolution of conflicts and disagreements in a positive and constructive manner.

"Consideration" behavior – A term used to describe the behavior of leaders/managers who show concern and consideration for subordinates and employees (also sometimes "employee-centered behavior").

Contingency Model (Fiedler) – See "Key concepts" below.

Continuum of Behavior (Tannenbaum & Schmidt) – See "Key concepts" below.

Flexible leadership – Openness to change and new information, adapting behavior and leadership methods in response.

Hierarchy of needs – Motivational theory developed by Abraham Maslow. See also Chapter 8 in *Leadership Express* in the *ExpressExec* series.

Influencing/negotiating – Persuading others, building consensus through give-and-take. Winning co-operation to accomplish goals and create a "win-win" situation.

Leader-member exchange theory – A model of leadership that focuses on the interaction between leaders and followers and the unique working relationships that develop. It accepts that leader and follower influence each other and as a result the subordinates negotiate their role in the organization. As the relationship develops, the subordinates gain more latitude. Nowadays, closely linked to concepts of empowerment.

Leadership Grid (Blake & Moulton) – See "Key concepts" below.

Management by objectives – A style of management or leadership in which subordinates are given goals and have to decide how to achieve them.

Path-Goal Theory (House) – See "Key concepts" below.

Situational Model (Blanchard & Hersey) – See "Key concepts" below.

Styles of leadership (Likert) – See "Key concepts" below.

Task orientation – An attitude or behavior of leaders/managers toward employees/subordinates that emphasizes task completion over concerns about their needs/wants (also sometimes "job-centered behavior").

Theory X and Theory Y – Motivational theory developed by Douglas McGregor: those who assume that people are lazy, dislike work, and will avoid it if they can, believe in Theory X. Those who believe in Theory Y assume that people are quite prepared to work and give of their best. See also Chapter 8 in *Leadership Express* in *ExpressExec* series.

Transactional leadership – See "Transformational versus transactional" below.

Transformational leadership – See "Transformational versus transactional" below and Chapter 6 in *Leadership Express* in the *ExpressExec* series.

Vision – A long-term view that pictures something different and better. Visionary leadership builds a shared vision with others and then enables them to translate it into reality.

Vroom-Yetton Decision Model – See "Key concepts" below.

KEY CONCEPTS

Styles of leadership

In the late 1940s, work on the subject of different leadership styles began at the University of Michigan. Rensis Likert published the results of these extensive studies in 1967. He identified four styles:

» *exploitative autocratic* – such leaders have neither trust nor confidence in their subordinates and act accordingly, issuing orders and putting pressure on performance;
» *benevolent autocratic* – the leader does have some trust in subordinates and so occasionally seeks their ideas and opinions, but the style is paternalistic;
» *participative* – with considerable trust and confidence, the leader frequently seeks subordinates' views and opinions, whilst retaining the ultimate decision-making power; and
» *democratic* – complete confidence and trust is displayed and the subordinates' views and opinions are not only sought but often acted upon.

Likert's research appeared to show that both participative and democratic styles were more successful than either of the autocratic styles. Subsequently the research has been criticized for not taking proper account of different situations – especially those where a more autocratic style may be essential, as in a crisis.

Continuum of Behavior

In 1957, Robert Tannenbaum and Warren Schmidt proposed a continuum which showed a range of behaviors that a leader, or manager, can adopt. It recognizes that the style chosen will depend on the leader's own personality, the personalities of colleagues, and the situation (e.g., time pressures, organizational culture).

At one end of the continuum is the use of authority, at the other increasing degrees of freedom for subordinates. There are seven behaviors.

1 The leader makes a decision and announces it.
2 The leader decides the appropriate action but "sells" it to subordinates.

3 The leader presents ideas and invites questions.
4 The leader presents a tentative decision but makes it subject to possible change.
5 The leader presents a problem, gets suggestions and ideas, and then makes a decision.
6 The leader defines the problem, allows subordinates to discuss it and make proposals, but the leader still makes the decision.
7 The leader defines the nature of the problem, explains the constraints and then joins in finding the solution.

Tannenbaum and Schmidt's model was updated in 1973 to reflect the growth of a more open style of leadership and as an acknowledgment that the leader was no longer likely to be the only holder of power.

The sort of factors that enable greater degrees of freedom and discretion to be given to subordinates include: their readiness to accept responsibility; their interest in the problem and their acknowledgment that solving it is important; and their level of knowledge and experience.

The Leadership Grid

In 1964, Robert Blake and Jane Moulton devised a grid that enabled them to define five leadership styles. Updated as recently as 1991, it uses two axes, calibrated 1–9, that measure a leader's concern for people on one axis and concern for task on the other. The five leadership behaviors are examined below.

Authority–obedience

This is an autocratic style used by the leader whose focus is fixed on completion of the task, with little concern for people. Procedures and directives determine what people should do and how they should do it. Such leaders drive their staff to maximize outputs.

Impoverished leadership

The laissez-faire leader, who is "semi-retired on the job." He or she has little concern for either the task or the people and only puts in the minimum effort required to keep the job running, but that is all.

Country club leadership

The leader whose focus is on people. Such leaders pay thoughtful attention to people's concerns, foster good feelings, create a comfortable friendly atmosphere, and minimize conflict, all with the expectation that people will get on and complete the job.

Middle-of-the-road leadership

Typically seen as the "organization man," the compromiser, keen to keep everyone happy. Because they are not strong on either task or people, they underachieve, failing to get the best out of people or their productive capacity.

Team leadership

High concern for both people and production. This leader is goal-centered but achieves results by obtaining the participation, involvement, and commitment of people.

Clearly the last of these styles is seen as an ideal. But some leaders switch styles depending on circumstances. Others wish to be perceived as "team leaders" but then accidentally display their real style which may be markedly different.

Blake and Moulton found that most people have a dominant style, with a back-up style ready if their usual style doesn't work in a particular situation.

Contingency Model

In 1967, Fred Fiedler sought to add situational variables to earlier work on leadership behaviors. In particular, he looked at three variables that should enable a leader to determine the most effective style:

» leader-member relationships – how well are they getting along, how well do they trust each other, and therefore how willing are they to follow the leader's directions? (possibilities: good or bad);
» nature of the task – is it well-structured, or dynamic and changing? (possibilities: structured or unstructured); and
» position power – how much authority or power does the leader have? (possibilities: high or low).

By combining all these possibilities, Fiedler came up with eight different situations – for example, a combination of good relations, structured task, and low power. From this he deduced which situations were very favorable, moderately favorable, and very unfavorable – an example of the latter being poor relations, unstructured task, and low power. He then looked at which leadership style – task- or people-oriented behavior – was appropriate for each situation.

What he concluded was that if the situation was highly unfavorable from the leader's perspective, then task-oriented behavior was best because a single-minded, driving approach was most likely to achieve the objective. Perhaps counter-intuitively, he decided that task orientation was also best when things were very favorable – lest everyone relaxed too much. In the middle ground, he proposed people-oriented behaviors because that was the point at which employee support and commitment would achieve most.

Fiedler's biggest contribution was to highlight the value of allowing people to maximize the fit between their style and the variables within the situation. It suggested that companies should analyze the situation and hire or promote the right person for the job.

Situational Model

Building on the earlier models of both Blake/Moulton and Fiedler (see above), Kenneth Blanchard and Paul Hersey created a Situational Model, the subject of their 1969 book *Management of Organizational Behavior: Leading Human Resources*, now in its eighth edition.

Although this book has sold a million copies worldwide, Blanchard is now much more famous for his 1982 bestseller *The One-Minute Manager*. With co-authors Patricia and Drea Zigarmi, he subsequently wrote *Leadership and the One-Minute Manager: Increasing Effectiveness Through Situational Leadership*, which currently stands at higher than 2500 in Amazon's rankings.

Hersey and Blanchard's approach took the same criteria as before – task and relationship (people) orientation. But, instead of taking all of Fiedler's variables, they picked subordinates' readiness to achieve the set task as the only variable. Readiness was defined as being willing *and/or* able or committed *and/or* competent. In each of four possible situations (i.e. subordinates being unable *and* unwilling or able *and* willing) a different leadership style was required.

» Telling/directing style – necessary when subordinates are unable (incompetent) and/or unwilling (uncommitted). They have to be told what is expected of them, and told what to do – a task orientation.
» Selling/coaching style – where subordinates have some competence but fairly low commitment, they need persuasion and coaching to achieve good results. This means concentrating on both task and relationship.
» Participating/supporting style – if there is high competence but a variable degree of commitment, the leader should play up the personal relationship aspects and avoid being too directive.
» Delegating style – if both competence and commitment are high, then the leader can happily adopt a delegating style. The leader facilitates rather than controls.

From a leader's viewpoint, it is clearly advantageous to develop subordinates so that they are both competent and committed, because delegation frees the leader's own time for other tasks and issues – common sense, but something well articulated by this model.

Path-Goal Theory

In the mid-1970s Robert House, currently Professor of Organizational Studies at the University of Pennsylvania's Wharton School, developed a model that took account of leader behavior and the motivation, performance, and satisfaction of followers or subordinates. House proposed that a leader could affect these by:

» offering rewards for achieving performance goals;
» clarifying paths towards these goals; and
» removing obstacles to performance.

He identified four styles of leadership behavior that achieve these objectives:

» directive leadership – the leader issues precise instructions and ground rules to the group and expects them to be followed;
» supportive leadership – a friendly approach that shows concern for subordinates' needs and wants;
» participative leadership – involves information sharing and seeking subordinates' views and ideas before decision making occurs; and

» achievement-oriented leadership – occurs when the leader sets subordinates challenging goals and expects high performance because the leader has confidence in the group's ability.

The model assumes that leaders are able to adapt their style according to the situation and therefore they need to take account of:

» the characteristics of the subordinates; and
» the demands or tasks facing them.

For example, if the group lacks confidence, then a supportive role is appropriate. If the task is ambiguous, then a more directive style is deemed best.

Vroom-Yetton Decision Model

This leader-participation model was originally created in 1973 by Victor Vroom, currently Professor of Organization and Management at Yale University's School of Management, and Philip Yetton, a professor at the Australia Graduate School of Management. Updated in 1988, by Vroom and Arthur Jago – currently a professor at the University of Missouri – this model is designed to help a leader choose how best to arrive at, communicate, and execute a decision. The following five styles are identified.

» Autocratic I – the leader solves the problem using information that is available to them at the time.
» Autocratic II – here, the leader obtains additional information from group members without necessarily discussing the problem, and then makes the decision alone. Group members may or may not be informed.
» Consultative I – the leader shares the problem with group members individually, and asks for information and evaluation. Group members do not meet collectively, and the leader makes the decision alone – one that may or may not reflect the advice received.
» Consultative II – leader shares the problem with group members collectively, but makes decision alone, again it may not reflect the group members' ideas.
» Group Consensus – leader meets with group to discuss situation. Leader focuses and directs discussion, but without imposing their

solution. Group makes final decision which is adhered to by the leader.

The choice of which style to adopt will depend on answering questions such as: How important is the technical quality of the decision? How important is my subordinates' commitment to the decision? Do I (the leader) have sufficient information to make a high quality decision on my own? Is the problem well structured (e.g., clearly defined, lends itself to a solution, has a time limit)? If I make the decision by myself, is it reasonably certain that my subordinates would commit to it? Do my subordinates have sufficient information to make a high quality decision? The answers to such questions – across 12 criteria – take the leader through a decision tree to arrive at the right conclusion.

Transformational versus transactional

In 1978, James MacGregor Burns' seminal book, *Leadership*, was published. In it, he distinguishes between transactional and transformational leadership.

Transactional leadership is what most people would recognize as management best practice, developed over the last half-century or so. It is transaction in the form of reciprocity, the idea that the relationship between leader and followers develops from the exchange of reward, such as performance-related pay, bonuses, promotion, recognition, and praise, in return for work well done.It means clear goals or objectives, well communicated and co-ordinated. It involves performance appraisal, job descriptions, and the delegation of responsibility.

MacGregor Burns, and others since, have seen this as no longer enough. Transactional leadership still presupposes hierarchy and a chain of command that cascades objectives. It assumes a leadership that controls through structures and processes to solve problems, plan, organize, and achieve results. Fair and process-oriented, it is still system-driven. Transactional leadership is "largely oriented toward accomplishing the tasks at hand and at maintaining good relations with those working with the leader."

Transformational leadership, on the other hand, is more about hearts and minds and empowering people rather than using rewards to (effectively) control them. Because transformation means change, such leadership is seen as releasing people to learn, to seek change and improvement. So it is based on trust on the part of the leader and understanding, skill, dedication, and commitment on the part of the followers. The transforming leader facilitates this.

Transformational leadership substitutes vision for objective. It relies on motivation that comes from a shared goal, not just a rewarded one. It stretches rather than delimits and rewards through a sense of involvement and achievement. It challenges rather than targets.

In MacGregor Burns' words, "transformational leadership refers to the process of influencing major changes in the attitudes and assumptions of organization members and building commitment for the organization's mission, objectives, and strategies." His thinking was therefore a big shift in emphasis, away from the more limited concepts of leadership developed by research up to this point. For more on transformational leadership, see Chapter 6 in *Leadership Express* in the *ExpressExec* series.

Action-Centered Leadership Model

The Action-Centered Leadership Model is a situational model pioneered by John Adair. Early in his career, Adair was Senior Lecturer in Military History and Advisor in Leadership Training at the Royal Military Academy, Sandhurst. He was appointed as the world's first Professor of Leadership Studies at Surrey University in the UK in 1978, and is currently Visiting Professor of Leadership Studies at the University of Exeter. He believes firmly that anyone taking charge of a team can develop leadership skills, but that these skills cannot be taught in isolation – they are learnt through (sometimes painful) experience.

Adair's approach to leadership is based on the use of authority appropriate to the situation. He defines four types of authority:

» position – "do this because I am boss;"
» knowledge – "authority flows to one who knows;"
» personality – in its extreme form this can include charisma; and
» moral authority – the personal authority to ask others to make sacrifices.

To get people to co-operate, a leader will need to understand the particular circumstances and choose which type of authority would be most effective. The leader who knows what to do inspires confidence in others, and this emphasizes the effect that technical and professional knowledge can have on a leader's development.

Adair's approach underlines the importance of group actions and teamwork. He believes that today leadership has a lot to do with team-work – the idea of a single great leader at the head of an organization is obsolete. A group of people working together develops a unique personality that has three overlapping areas of need: to achieve the task; to build and maintain the team; and to develop the individual. Because each interacts with the others, if a task is achieved, the team develops and individuals are satisfied. Similarly, if a group lacks cohesion then its task performance will fall with a consequent drop in individual morale.

Good leaders have full command of these three areas and use each of the elements within them, according to the situation and the people involved. Achieving the task requires defining what is involved, planning how to tackle it and allocating the work. Once work starts, it needs controlling and monitoring while performance is evaluated. If necessary, the plan is adjusted. Building and maintaining the team means creating a sense of purpose, giving a clear briefing, setting standards, leading by example, building team spirit, motivating, and communicating. Leaders need to support their team, offering encouragement, recognizing success, and learning from failures. In terms of developing the individual, leaders need to recognize and use each individual's abilities, advise, listen, enthuse, provide good training, and be attentive to anyone's personal problems.

The ability to inspire people is part of leadership and people can find this daunting – especially if they feel that they have to display charis-matic inspiration. Adair believes that it is perfectly possible to inspire others by setting an example, showing enthusiasm, commitment, and integrity, and by combining this with an ability to communicate feelings and emotions rather than just cold facts.

Resources

Thousands of articles and books include ideas and prescriptions for successful leadership styles. Chapter 9 looks at some of the better sources for those who want to know more (with Websites where appropriate):

» online resources for checking personality types;
» some leadership centers;
» specialist sources; and
» relevant books.

"Life is more than just reaching our goals. As individuals and as a group we need to reach our potential. Nothing else is good enough. We must always be reaching toward our potential"

Max DePree, author of The Art of Leadership

Anyone looking for more resources on leadership styles will have plenty to choose from – Websites, books, magazines, and much else besides. For example, a Google search on "leadership [or] styles" produces just under 300,000 hits. If you refine the search to the exact phrase "leadership styles" (which of course excludes "styles of leadership") it comes down to a mere 31,000! Well short of the six million hits you get on "leadership" alone, but plenty to be going on with ... What follows is guidance on where to find some of the most useful resources that you may want to reach for.

PERSONALITY TYPES

In Chapter 2 we mentioned the Myers – Briggs Type Indicator® – MBTI®. The product of a remarkable endeavor between a mother, Katharine Cook Briggs, and her daughter, Isabel Briggs Myers, that first began in the 1940s. KnowYourType was the first company to offer this instrument online. You can find them at http://www.knowyourtype.com/. For individuals the cost is $99, for companies the price is discounted depending on the number of users. If you just want more information, you can find out about the eight alternative personal preferences and the 16 personality types that the test reveals. For fun, you can check out what type famous people are – Bill Gates and Margaret Thatcher are the same, as are Elvis Presley and Elizabeth Taylor. The only problem is that some of the "famous" people have been dead a long while – Queen Elizabeth I and George Washington, for example. So there's a good bit of guessing going on!

TEAM ROLES

Dr R. Meredith Belbin, while teaching at Henley Management College in England, noticed that some teams of students worked well together and others didn't. It appeared to have little to do with intelligence or ability. He therefore began a nine-year study looking into what was going on, before identifying nine different team roles. Whilst not strictly about leadership styles, the Belbin® Team Roles Indicator will show you your preferred style within a team (e.g. chairman, etc.).

To find out more, you can visit http://www.belbin.com/ where, for £25 (about $15), you can have the questionnaire sent to you (in PDF format) by e-mail. If you want to know more about the roles, you'll find plenty of information on the Website.

Another, more recent, indicator of preferred team roles is the Management Team Roles Indicator – MTR-i™ . Although MTR-i™ is trademarked by S.P. Myers, there is no family relationship with Isabel Myers! But there does appear to be a tie-in between the MBTI® personality types and MTR-I™ preferred roles – perhaps not surprising since they are both based on Jung's psychological types. Find out more about all of these at http://www.teamtechnology.co.uk/, where there are all sorts of comparisons.

One other area worth investigating is the Enneagram Institute at http://www.enneagraminstitute.com/home.asp. Though go to FAQs to learn the origin of Enneagram before going further. For wider comment on the subject, give it a Google search – you'll find about 70,000 pages!

BROADER RESOURCES

One of the most valuable resources is the Peter Drucker Foundation (http://www.pfdf.org). Although this is primarily intended for non-profit management, it is a great resource for anyone interested in leadership. Not least because it publishes a quarterly journal, *Leader to Leader*, with articles written by leaders from both academic and business communities as well as respected social thinkers.

On its Website you can find extracts from relevant books and, most importantly, many articles previously published in *Leader to Leader*. These are freely available, going back to 1996 – see http://www.pfdf.org/leaderbooks/l2l/index.html. Here you will find articles by Herb Kelleher, Warren Bennis, Peter Senge, Peter Drucker, Rosabeth Moss Kanter, Max DePree, and many more.

As you might expect, Ohio State University (see Chapters 3 and 8) has its own Leadership Center although, surprisingly, it only started in 1990. It has a quarterly publication called *Leadership Link*, started in 1996, which is offered both in printed form and online. You can also subscribe to their weekly e-mail *Leadership Moments* (very short, one-page thought-provokers) or *Leadership Discoveries*, which comes out monthly and is slightly longer. Go to http://www.ag.ohio-state.edu/~leaders/.

Robert House (see Chapters 3 and 8) is at the University of Pennsylvania's Wharton Business School, which has a Center for Leadership and Change Management. The Center has published a monthly *Leadership Digest* since 1996, and all articles from all issues are available online at no cost – see http://leadership.wharton.upenn.edu/welcome/index.shtml.

Housed at the University of Maryland is the James MacGregor Burns Academy of Leadership. It goes well beyond business leadership, targeting "groups historically under-represented in public life." But it is an important think-tank, training center, and educational institution all rolled into one. They have a wealth of papers and articles available on the Website (under "publications") – http://www.academy.umd.edu/publications/index.htm – including the Kellogg Leadership Studies Project Working Papers. Or start at the beginning at http://www.academy.umd.edu/home/index.htm.

The Council for Management and Leadership Excellence (CEML) is a UK-based council established in April 2000 by the government's Department of Trade & Industry and Department for Education & Skills. Its purpose is to draw up a strategy for management and leadership development to ensure that the UK has the managers and leaders of the future "to match the best in the world."

Given the significance of the small and medium-sized enterprise sector (SMEs), its publication *Management and Leadership in UK SMEs: Witness Accounts from the World of Entrepreneurs and SME Managers* may be of interest. All CEML's publications are available for free download at http://www.managementandleadershipcouncil.org/index.htm.

CEML has also published *Leadership Development: Best Practice Guide for Organisations*. This is now available as an interactive online tool to help users review their organization against best practice and develop an appropriate action plan. You can find this at http://194.202.64.171/8531_CEML/.

SPECIALIST SOURCES

For those who find the growing interest in servant leadership interesting, there are many available resources. The first is bound to be http://www.greenleaf.org/. The Robert K. GreenleafCenter for Servant-Leadership was originally founded in 1964 as the Center for Applied Ethics, Inc., and was renamed in 1985. It is an international, not-for-profit institution headquartered in Indianapolis. Its online resource catalogue offers a complete collection of Greenleaf's work as well as dozens of books and videos by leading thinkers and practitioners in the art of leadership. There's also plenty to read online at http://www.greenleaf.org/leadership/read-about-it/Servant-Leadership-Articles-Book-Reviews.html.

Since it is the *Fortune* "100 Best Companies to Work for" that most recently highlighted the potential power of servant leadership, you can check out the list at: http://www.fortune.com/indexw.jhtml?channel=list.jhtml&list_frag=list_3column_best_companies_work_for.jhtml&list=5&_requestid=72. To look at one of the companies and their commitment to this style of leadership, go to http://www.tdindustries.com/AboutUs/ServantLeadership.asp

There are also lots of references to follow-up in a paper given at a Servant Leadership Symposium in 2000. It can be found at British Colombia Trinity Western University's Website: http://www.twu.ca/leadership/articles/meaning.htm.

Max DePree founded the DePree Leadership Center in 1996. With forty years of corporate experience, DePree is chairman emeritus of Herman Miller, Inc., and a member of *Fortune* magazine's National Business Hall of Fame. He is also a member of the advisory board of the Peter F. Drucker Foundation (see above). His books on leadership include *Leadership Is an Art*, *Leadership Jazz*, and *Leading Without Power*.

The DePree Leadership Center takes a greater interest in the spiritual side of leadership than the Greenleaf Center. It can be found at http://www.depree.org/depree/.

If Konosuke Matsushita's philosophy is of interest, then there are interesting resources at http://www.matsushita.co.jp/corp/rekishikan/index_e.html. Nine of his books can also be ordered direct from http://www.php.co.jp/japaninface/bookorder.html.

BOOKS

There are many books that can provide a good resource.

Collected works

Among the books available are two collections of essays:

» *The Leader of The Future* – published by the Peter F. Drucker Foundation (see above) in 1996. This book has a collection of essays by selected thought-leaders. It includes the thinking of Stephen Covey, Ken Blanchard, Ed Schein, Sally Helgesen, and Peter Senge, among many others; and

» *The Future of Leadership* – more recent, published in 2001 by Jossey-Bass. This collection of essays includes Warren Bennis among its editors. Contributors include Bennis himself, Edward Lawler, Charles Handy, Thomas Davenport, Tom Peters, James Kouzes, and Barry Posner.

Role models

In terms of role models, there are two books that look at a variety of leaders:

» *The New Global Leaders* by Manfred Kets de Vries – published by Jossey-Bass in 1999, this book provides some excellent insights into three leaders that Kets de Vries identifies as global leaders: Richard Branson of Virgin, Percy Barnevik of ABB, and David Simon of BP (see Chapter 7).

» *21 Leaders for the 21st Century* by Fons Trompenaars and Charles Hampden-Turner – published by Capstone in 2001, this book lets the authors (see Chapter 5) describe and develop their concept of "transcultural competence." In it, they interview and recount the story of 21 leaders, including: Philippe Bourguignon (see Chapter 5), now at Club Med; Michael Dell of Dell Computers; Karel Vuursteen of Heineken; and Anders Knutsen of Bang & Olufsen.

Of course, if you want to really enjoy yourself, then get *Nuts!*, the story of Herb Kelleher and Southwest Airlines as told by Kevin and Jackie Freiberg – published in hardback in 1996 by Bard Press and in paperback by Broadway in 1998. It is an amazing and funny story! Or, visit Southwest's own Website to get a flavor. Start at http://www.iflyswa.com/about_swa/airborne.html.

For a much more detailed history of Konosuke Matsushita, then try *Matsushita Leadership: Lessons from the 20th Century's Most Remarkable Entrepreneur* (Free Press, 1997) by John P. Kotter, himself the Konosuke Matsushita Professor of Leadership at Harvard Business School – a post resulting from just one of the three $1mn endowments that Matsushita made to US universities and business schools.

Particular themes

If you want to know more about emotional intelligence (and you should), then Daniel Goleman's first book *Emotional Intelligence* is now available in paperback (Bantam, 1997, reprint edition), though his follow-up *Working with Emotional Intelligence* may be even more relevant. It came out in paperback in 2000 (also by Bantam). Worth getting hold of, if it's easy, is Goleman's article "What makes a Leader?" published in *Harvard Business Review*, November–December, 1998.

If you want to know more about women and leadership, you can download Judy Rosener's original 1990 *Harvard Business Review* article, "Ways Women Lead," as a PDF file at amazon.com for $6 (see Chapter 6). Her 1997 book, *America's Competitive Secret: Women Managers*, is published by Oxford University Press.

Sally Helgesen's book, *The Female Advantage: Women's Ways of Leadership*, (see Chapter 6) was republished in 1995 by Currency/Doubleday and her more recent book, *The Web of Inclusion*, was published in the same year by the same publishers. It looks in depth at five companies, including the *Miami Herald*, Intel, and Nickelodeon.

If Rob Goffee and Gareth Jones' ideas (see Chapter 6) about the different types of organizations people are called upon to lead whetted your appetite to know more, their book, *The Character of the Corporation*, was published by HarperCollins Business in 1998.

Fons Trompenaars and Charles Hampden-Turner's book, *Riding The Waves of Culture: Understanding Diversity in Global Business*, was published by McGraw-Hill in the US and Nicholas Brealey in Europe. Their earlier book, *The Seven Cultures of Capitalism*, published in 1993, is now unfortunately out of print. But *Building Cross-Cultural Competence: How to Create Wealth from Conflicting*

Values, published in 2000, by Yale University Press in the US and John Wiley & Sons Ltd in the rest of the world, is an update on their growing research base. For another take on culture, try *Culture's Consequences: Comparing Values, Behaviors, Institutions and Organizations Across Nations*, by longstanding cultural guru Geert Hofstede – its second edition was published in 2001 by Sage Publications.

The detailed views of Patricia Pitcher – who has classified leaders into three categories (see Chapter 2) – can be found in *The Drama of Leadership*, published by John Wiley & Sons in 1997.

Ken Blanchard (see Chapters 3 and 8) is a highly prolific writer and well-known for his *One-Minute Manager* series of books. Many look at motivation, empowerment, coaching, and teams. With co-authors Patricia and Drea Zigarmi, he wrote *Leadership and the One-Minute Manager: Increasing Effectiveness Through Situational Leadership*, which is due out in paperback in early 2002. If you want a slim book with just some key leadership ideas, try *The Heart of a Leader*. This has 76 quotes (on the left-hand pages) and Blanchard's explanations of them (on the right-hand pages).

John Adair is another prolific writer, his books include *The John Adair Handbook of Management and Leadership*, published by Hawksmere Ltd in 1998, and *Not Bosses but Leaders: How to Lead the Way to Success*, published by Kogan Page in 1990. His most recent book is *John Adair's 100 Greatest Leadership Ideas*, published by Capstone in 2001.

General

There are a number of books that anyone interested in leadership and leadership styles would do well to read. Among those to be recommended are *Hidden Value: How Great Companies Achieve Extraordinary Results with Ordinary People*, by two professors at Stanford University, Charles O'Reilly and Jeffrey Pfeffer. The book contains a profile of the management practices of seven highly successful companies, including Southwest Airlines, Cisco Systems, The SAS Institute, and The Men's Wearhouse. The focus is on unleashing the power of people's hearts and minds.

Another book, with a similar title, is *The Leadership Challenge: How to Keep Getting Extraordinary Things Done in Organizations*, by James Kouzes and Barry Posner. Reprinted as a second edition by Jossey-Bass in 1996, the book has sold 750,000 copies. The two authors have subsequently produced *The Leadership Challenge Planner: An Action Guide to Achieving Your Personal Best*, designed to be a workbook and stand-alone self-learning tool. If having to read too many books is a problem, you can always buy a 16-page (yes, 16!) booklet called *The Five Practices of Exemplary Leadership: When Leaders Are at Their Best*, by Kouzes and Posner, in which they encapsulate their five main themes. It costs $10 and is produced by Jossey-Bass.

A book designed for use on leadership courses that covers a lot of good ground is *Understanding Behaviors for Effective Leadership*, by Jon Howell and Dan Costley, and published by Prentice Hall in 2000. It has a strong emphasis on different behaviors and their appropriateness for different situations. It describes seven leadership types: supportive, directive, participative, transactional, charismatic, network, and relationship leaders.

Overall

A recently published book that is highly recommended is *The Leadership Mystique: a user's guide for the human enterprise*, by Manfred Kets de Vries. Published in autumn 2001, it covers emotional intelligence, effective leadership, the roots of failure, global leadership, and many other subjects that are critical to the subject. Clearly written, it is full of good self-check questions (as opposed to the often awful ones found in other books). "Organizations," in Kets de Vries' view, "are like automobiles. They don't run themselves, except downhill." For a big view of leadership, this book, from one of Europe's best management thinkers, is a good place to start.

Ten Steps to Making Your Leadership Style Work

There is no magic formula for a successful leadership style, but there are a number of lessons that are important and will improve the likelihood of success. Chapter 10 includes the following steps:

- » know and be yourself;
- » listen and learn;
- » communicate;
- » adaptability, flexibility;
- » no style without substance;
- » competencies, competencies, competencies;
- » keep developing your "EQ";
- » care for people *and* the job;
- » set the example; and
- » get the best out of people.

"You've got to do your own growing, no matter how tall your grandfather is."

Irish proverb

One thing that should be clear by now is that there is no universal leadership style that works in all situations. There is no set of traits that can endow someone with a predisposition to have the right leadership style – though there may be some characteristics that suit certain circumstances well. Indeed, leadership itself can be difficult to define because of its elusive nature.

So, if one is cast in a leadership role, how does one respond? What can be done to develop a really effective leadership style? Clearly, at the stage this is likely to happen, much of one's personality and character is already formed. What, then, are the steps that can be taken?

There is no magic formula, though there are plenty who would try to prescribe one. There are instead a number of lessons, drawn from all the work on leadership styles, that taken together should improve one's style of leadership and therefore its effectiveness. Here are ten of them.

1. KNOW AND BE YOURSELF

There can be little doubt that the most important thing is to know yourself. Style is about behavior, attitudes, and motivation. These in turn are reflections of our personality and character; of the way we think and feel – complex reactions formed by our instinct and experience.

Because these are often unconscious processes, we need to set time aside to understand them. What drives us? What makes us do things in a certain way? Why do we react the way we do? These aren't easy questions, but failing to ask them will leave us blind to what may be critical strengths or weaknesses in our style.

It also means that we have a weak understanding of how far we can adapt our style without moving too far outside our real character. It becomes all to easy to adopt a style that is expected of us, rather than one which suits our temperament and values so that, before we know it, we become what Kets de Vries describes as a "false self" (see Chapter 2).

Once we know ourselves, we are able to be ourselves – the critical part of being able to act with integrity. We can also go on learning. We are each so complex that we cannot ever fully understand ourselves and we continue to gain experience – sometimes character-forming experience – that creates further shifts in who we are. That is why we should regularly hold a mirror up and take a good look at ourselves.

One of the ways to begin this process is to take one of the personality tests that are widely available (see Chapters 2 and 9). Getting feedback on the type of person we are is a valuable starting point, it helps us to understand how others see us and even why we find other types easy or hard to work with, and especially to lead.

2. LISTEN AND LEARN

It is widely held that leadership can be learnt. So, too, can many attributes of an effective leadership style. And high on the priority list is the ability to listen. Not just passively, but actively. Not just hearing audible signals, but listening in its broadest sense.

A great deal of good leadership is about being able to judge and sum up situations accurately. Many effective leaders are seen to be able to do this almost instinctively. Whereas, in fact, what they have done is develop the ability to pick up not just what is being said, but also the way it is said. They listen for nuance, for subtle clues. They pick up non-verbal communication. They sense changes in mood or atmosphere. They really "listen."

All of this is learnable. It takes work and conscious effort. But once we begin to enhance our abilities, the rewards are clear. We diminish the likelihood of stumbling into a situation we did not expect, we improve our chances of foreseeing what is happening and therefore of being able to act appropriately.

In what seems like an uncanny replay of what happened at BP with Robert Horton and David Simon (see Chapter 7), Jac Nasser has recently been removed as CEO of Ford Motor Company after three years in the job. Henry Ford's great-grandson, Bill Ford, has taken over as CEO, as well as remaining chairman, and brought in Englishman Nick Scheele as chief operating officer. Although Ford had been suffering severe financial problems, the changes had a good deal to do with leadership style.[1] On the day of the announcement, Bill Ford told a meeting of employees that the new team had "an eagerness to listen to all of you" and that part of his focus would be on "rebuilding relationships." Nick Scheele pointed out that "the employees know we've got an awful lot of restructuring to do, but they also want to be listened to. To move forward, we must have full team support."

A leader's ability to listen – and learn – is critical.

3. COMMUNICATE

But listening is only one half of a bigger process: two-way communication. Another essential leadership skill that can be learnt is the ability to communicate clearly but with sensitivity to the situation. Leaders need to say what they mean and mean what they say. And they need to be consistent. Nobody can try to achieve an unarticulated goal, no one commits to a badly communicated vision. Leaders have to communicate in a way that others understand.

But *how* things are communicated is also vital. Just as listening isn't simply about hearing, effective communication is not just about putting something into written or spoken words. We all communicate all the time in the way we behave and act. And nothing gives the wrong signals more than saying one thing and doing another. It shatters credibility and undermines integrity – both fatal to the cause of effective leadership. As Warren Bennis says, "leadership is first being, then doing. Everything the leader does reflects what he or she is."[2]

4. ADAPTABILITY, FLEXIBILITY

The danger of underlining the need for consistency in what we do and say is that it can be seen as a straitjacket. Good leaders remain adaptable and flexible to different situations. They know there is a difference between underlying consistency and rigid inflexibility. They have core values that they stick to and an underlying goal they are seeking to achieve, but they don't have a "one style fits all" approach.

Whether it is at the macro or micro level, they show their flexibility, responding as circumstances demand. The world is littered with leaders who have failed because they applied a style of leadership, that worked in one environment, to another, different one. They rewind the tape and play it again, irrespective of the new context. Famously, generals always fight the last war!

Jack Welch, the legendary, blunt CEO of GE, who retired in 2001, is seen as an archetypal effective leader – see Chapter 7 in *Leadership Express* in the *ExpressExec* series. Soon after his appointment in 1980, he set a fundamental criterion for all of GE's businesses. They would have to be either number one or two in their competitive global markets. Those that had no chance of achieving this were "to be fixed – sold – or closed."

Some 15 years later he listened to members of a mid-level company training program as they pointed out that this central tenet – to be number one or two in its markets – was losing GE vital business, because business heads were narrowing their market definitions in order to achieve that positioning. Not only did Welch listen, but he immediately ensured that in future they define their markets so that they had a market share of 10% or less. What he described as "this punch in the nose" from middle managers, and his willingness to see it as a "better idea," was a big factor in GE's double-digit revenue growth in the second half of the 1990s.

5. NO STYLE WITHOUT SUBSTANCE

Another danger is that, by emphasizing "style," there is a suggestion that leadership is no more than that. Nothing could be further from the truth. Leadership is nothing without substance, nor is style. Leadership requires a wide range of abilities, skills, and values. Warren Bennis puts it well: "competence, or knowledge, without vision and virtue breeds technocrats. Virtue, without vision and knowledge, breeds ideologues. Vision, without virtue and knowledge, breeds demagogues."[3]

But, to be successful, it also requires business or organizational acumen. Herb Kelleher of Southwest Airlines (see Chapter 7) is known for his colorful leadership style, a reputation he relishes. However, nobody should doubt he isn't a conscientious and highly skilled businessman. Among his tenets are:

» "manage in the good times for the bad times" – don't get fat and complacent, keep your eye constantly on costs;

» "take the competition, but not yourself, seriously" – never take your eye off what your competitors are doing;
» "think of your company as a service organization that happens to be in the airline business" – service business depends on customer service, so that is the focus, and the way you treat your employees is the way they will treat your customers; and
» "think small to grow big" – success comes in attention to detail.

So, while the US was enjoying its prolonged boom in the late 1990s, and Kelleher was cracking jokes in public, he was quietly taking Southwest's costs down by 10% to be ready for any hard times around the corner. Good leaders develop consummate management skills to fit alongside their chosen leadership style.

6. COMPETENCIES, COMPETENCIES, COMPETENCIES

As Manfred Kets de Vries says, "in any given situation, a certain set of competencies contribute to effective leadership. The challenge for leaders (or potential leaders) is to develop a repertoire of competencies that covers most contingencies." This is lifelong learning.

The more competencies we can build up, the better our leadership style will be. But there isn't a structured course. We have to learn and practice, observe and gain from experience. Even those who have been in leadership roles for some time should put themselves on regular personal refresher courses. It is astonishingly easy to hunker down into a repetitive style.

What, though, are some of the things to try? Here are some basic ones.

» Practice asking open-ended questions – they provide a freer range of expression, create listening opportunities, and can uncover misunderstandings. Established leaders can lose this skill.
» Be specific – try making your comments and remarks as plain and down-to-earth as possible. Notice when and if you've absorbed buzzwords into your vocabulary. Kill them or make sure you explain them properly.
» Challenge stereotypes – both your own and everyone else's. This is a huge area for exploration. Many corporate cultures have all

sorts of stereotypes – from classic successes to stupendous failures: "remember the 'XYZ' project, this is the same." Challenge them. In doing so, you may well find they are not stereotypical and you assert your own right (and duty) to question. From a cultural perspective (see Chapter 5), this challenging is critical – blaming cultural differences is far too easily (and often) done. Established leaders can fall victim to a conventional wisdom.

» Check assumptions – they are often wrong. "Never assume anything" is an excellent motto and, if you're listening well, you can hear them coming up, even if they aren't framed as "I assume that . . . "

» Break habits – "the way we do things round here" is both a strength and a weakness. It can be culturally binding, but may also prevent forward movement and change. Put a shock into the system by intentionally varying something that has become habitual.

» Give honest feedback – because it may be uncomfortable, we often find excuses for avoiding it. Practice it, and find ways to move on to coaching and mentoring.

These are just a few examples of the way we can check our behavior and re-learn. The more we experience, the more we gain in competence. The more competencies we gain, the better our leadership style can become.

7. KEEP DEVELOPING YOUR "EQ"

Leadership is not just a cerebral activity – logic and reason have their place but there is much more to it than that. Acknowledging that it is not all rational is a major step toward accepting that there is something else – people's feelings and emotion. To win commitment, these have to be engaged.

Self-knowledge is the first step toward developing emotional intelligence (see Step 1 above). The next step is to learn how to manage our own emotions – finding ways to control our anger or frustration rather than let them burst out. Outbursts of anger may appear to have an effect on people, but it is the effect of fear and, in the long run, is deeply demotivating. Anger can instead be channeled into self-motivation, to look at why something has gone wrong and then to correct it without simply blaming others.

The third stage in developing emotional intelligence is to learn how to recognize and handle other people's emotions. The ability to empathize – to understand how others may feel – is something we can learn. It's not easy, particularly if we are rather self-centered ourselves, but by putting effort into it we can start to see how the world looks through someone else's eyes. This is a critical key to motivating people – an essential for an effective leadership style.

8. CARE FOR PEOPLE AND THE JOB

Nowadays, there is a great deal of emphasis in leadership on caring for people. As many of the earlier points underline, this is a critical element. But it is also vital to concentrate on what needs to be done, the task at hand. The job of a leader is to achieve a goal – that is the end, leading people is the means.

The examples of successful leadership styles in Chapter 7 reinforce this. David Simon was a caring leader who took people with him, but he never once took his eye off what he was trying to achieve. Konosuke Matsushita introduced all sorts of innovative idea in terms of winning commitment from his people, but he also demanded that targets were met, that customers were respected, and that both quality and productivity were constantly improved. He cared for both people *and* the job. Herb Kelleher is no different – he "loves" the people at Southwest Airlines but, as illustrated above, he also focuses on costs, the competition, and the quality of service the company provides.

9. SET THE EXAMPLE

It is a fundamental part of good leadership that the leader has to set an example. It is therefore a critical element in leadership style. Everything about our style of leadership should personify what we expect from others. Robert Horton at BP (see Chapter 7) talked of empowerment and teams but did not "live" it himself. David Simon literally did what he promoted, he was open, approachable, empowering, and actively worked as a team player.

If you want trust, then trust people yourself. If you want to encourage honesty, be honest yourself. Leaders often forget that their every action and word is under a microscope. Leadership is usually a highly exposed position and any mismatch between what is said and done is quickly visible. Ensure your leadership style sets the example for everyone else.

10. GET THE BEST OUT OF PEOPLE

Leaders need to understand that at the heart of what they are trying to do is getting the best out of people. Time was when it was about getting the best out of a machine, but not any more. What a leader achieves today depends on the people they are leading, and the best way to win is to get them to give of their best. Everything in our leadership style should be focused toward this end.

In 1979, Konosuke Matsushita gave an incredibly blunt assessment of what was wrong with Western businesses. He blamed the deeply embedded residue of Frederick Winslow Taylor's "scientific management" (see Chapter 1) that still affects the way many organizations run. It bears repeating here as a final sanity check on our own attitudes and leadership style:

"Your firms are built on the Taylor model; even worse, so are your heads. With your bosses doing the thinking while the workers wield the screwdrivers, you're convinced deep down that this is the right way to run a business. For you, the essence of management is getting the ideas out of the heads of bosses and into the hands of labor."

"We are beyond the Taylor model. Business, we know, is now so complex and difficult, the survival of firms so hazardous in an environment increasingly unpredictable, competitive, and fraught with danger, that their continued existence depends on the day-to-day mobilization of every ounce of intelligence."

"For us, the core of management is precisely this art of mobilizing and pulling together the intellectual resources of all employees in the service of the firm. Because we have measured better than you the scope of the new technological and economic challenges, we know that the intelligence of a handful of technocrats, however brilliant and smart they may be, is no longer enough to stand a real chance of success. Only by drawing on the combined brainpower of all its employees, can a firm face up to the turbulence and constraints of today's environment."

Make sure your leadership style is designed to bring out the best in your people.

NOTES

1 *Financial Times*, October 31, 2001.
2 Warren Bennis, *On Becoming a Leader*.
3 *Ibid.*

Frequently Asked Questions (FAQs)

Q1: Is there a set of personal traits that creates the right leadership style?

A: Our personal traits play a large part in the style we can adopt, but as Chapter 3 shows, there is no one set of universal traits that leads to a successful style.

Q2: Is a more feminine leadership style more appropriate these days?

A: There are certainly those who argue the case. The research discussed in Chapter 6 suggests there are differences between feminine and masculine styles, but appropriateness depends on the situation.

Q3: Is there one leadership style that works best?

A: No. All the research discussed in Chapter 3 underlines that there is no universally successful style, it all depends on the circumstances. The examples of three successful, but different, leadership styles in Chapter 7 proves the point.

Q4: How much does our personality determine the right leadership style?

A: A good deal. As is explained in Chapter 2, the way we behave and act is heavily determined by our character and personality. To act out-of-character can be unproductive, if not downright dangerous.

Q5: Do different organizations need different styles?

A: Yes. We explain in Chapter 6 why, just as organizations differ, so do the styles they need. As the example of Robert Horton in Chapter 7 shows, even different parts of the same organization can respond differently to a leadership style.

Q6: Isn't getting the job done more important than worrying about people?

A: As the research in Chapter 8 and the examples in Chapter 7 show, good leaders care about both. Leaders are judged by the goals they achieve, but they can only achieve those goals through people.

Q7: Do people from different cultures have different leadership styles?

A: Yes they do. As we explain in Chapter 5, cultural differences play a large part in how leaders behave and in what people expect of their leader. Understanding this is critical to cross-cultural leadership.

Q8: Are there situations where you have to just tell people what to do?

A: Yes. As explained in Chapter 8, there can be a number of situations where being directive is the appropriate leadership style. There are also circumstances where it is highly inappropriate.

Q9: I've heard about "servant leadership" – what is it?

A: It is a style of leadership that is growing in use, as explained in Chapter 6. Herb Kelleher, CEO of Southwest Airlines, is a "servant leader" – see Chapter 7.

Q10: How do I choose the right leadership style?

A: By understanding what it involves, as explained in Chapter 2, and by recognizing the importance of judging the situation in which it is to be used – see Chapters 6 and 8.

Acknowledgments

Disneyland® is a registered trademark of Disney Enterprises, Inc.

MBTI®, Myers – Briggs Type Indicator®, and Myers – Briggs® are registered trademarks of Consulting Psychologists Press, Inc.

Belbin® is a registered trademark of Belbin Associates.

MTR-i™ (Management Team Roles Indicator) is a registered trademark of S.P. Myers.

Index